Praise for **Mermaid In The Mountains**

"*'Mermaid In The Mountains'* draws you in with

such **artistry** and **feeling** . . . I am right

beside her on the **journey**. I **loved** it!"

—*Reiki Master, MARY ROSE D.*

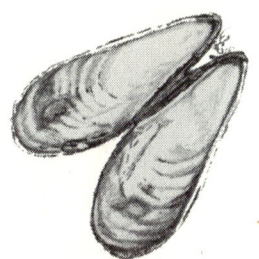

"**Enchanting** . . . I **loved** it!"

—*MTPR host, JOHN A.*

"A **heralding** call to us all to find the

joy between the lines."

—*Jeweler, CHELSEY B.*

"A **laugh** out loud quick read . . .

Fantastic!"

—*VA nurse, TINA A.*

"**Captures** the **wonder**

and **beauty** of life!"

—*Artisan, OTELIA B.*

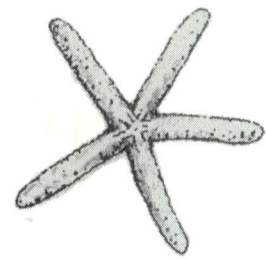

Mermaid IN THE
MOUNTAINS

A HUMOROUS, HARROWING, AND HEARTWARMING TALE
OF ENDING UP IN THE LEAST LIKELY OF PLACES,
AND FINDING OUT IT'S EXACTLY WHERE YOU BELONG

C.M. ARVISH

Inspirational   Nonfiction

THE COLORFUL QUILL    amazonkindle

Published by THE COLORFUL QUILL
in association with amazonkindle

MERMAID IN THE MOUNTAINS © 2018 by C.M. Arvish

Paperback ISBN: 9780-578-21523-5
eBook ISBN: 9780-578-21522-8

Library of Congress Cataloging-in-Publication Data
Arvish, Carrie Malia
Mermaid In The Mountains/Carrie Malia Arvish
    1.   Missoula, Montana — Nonfiction
          TXu 2-106-709   2018

First Paperback and ebook editions published 2019 Rev. 4

Image Credits
Shutterstock images used for cover and title page
Original artwork by C.M. Arvish

This book is dedicated with love to "you,"
Boo, and a Menehune or two.

A note from the author

Some of the names have been changed, except for a couple of instances, to protect the good, the bad, and the oddly eccentric.

A big mahalo to the great Hawaiian tradition of "talk story," where people at luaus, and around campfires throughout the islands, laugh at each other's follies, comfort the sorrows, and celebrate the victories. (Some valleys and sacred sites have been altered or moved to disguise their exact locations).

I feel honored to have been raised around Northwest Coast First Nations people, and Polynesian storytellers who delighted, taught, and entertained people.

These stories are exactly how I remember them, but I pre-apologize if there are any, as my dad likes to say, "Creative memories" within this book's pages. If there are, we can blame it on the Menehunes.

This book has been made especially for you, with heart and soul.

CONTENTS

{Mokuna 1}

The Evil Doer and Early Hawaii

{Mokuna 2}

An Island of Another Kind

{Mokuna 3}

Adventures in Paradise

{Mokuna 4}

Harrowing Leaps and Crazy Kayakers

{Mokuna 5}

A Horse of Course

{Mokuna 6}

Princess Papouli and a Mid-day Moon

{Mokuna 7}

Hippies and Angels

{Mokuna 8}

I Left My Little Island

{Mokuna 9}

Monkeys and Dying Elephant

{Mokuna 10}

He-Who-Shall-Not-be-Named, Escorts Me to Italy

{Mokuna 11}

Quicker than a Las Vegas Wedding

{Mokuna 12}

It Happened

{Mokuna 13}

Three Horse Town

{Mokuna 14}

Pixie-Haired Monster and the Lovely Red House

{Mokuna 15}

Tupelo Honey

{Mokuna 16}

Frankenstein Holes and a Frog Fish

{Mokuna 17}

Three More Months with My Last Name

{Mokuna 18}

I Do

{Mokuna 19}

I Do Too

{Mokuna 20}

Grandpas; Almost Near the End

Mermaid IN THE
MOUNTAINS

Ala: a road, path, or trail, watchful and alert.

Lokahi: harmony and unity.

Oia'i'o: truthful and honest.

Ha'aha'a: unassuming and humble.

Ahonui: having patience and perseverance.

Mokuna 1: **The Evil Doer and Early Hawaii**

I climbed into the shower, as I was instructed to do.

"Take a hot and cold shower," he said, "it's only your nerves waking up."

I desperately tried, but crumbled to my knees, facing the wall as I braced myself on trembling arms, the increasing horror and pain of what was happening to me piercing my mind. I barely climbed out of the shower, unable to towel myself off, and ended up belly down on the bathroom floor, naked, eyes closed, hardly able to move; in so much pain I did not know how I would survive.

There was no way I could have known in that horrible moment that I was going to be held in hands much greater than my own, transported to a place I couldn't have imagined, and given some of my life's greatest treasures.

He stood back, an ominous presence blocking the doorway, as I was lying on the hard, unforgiving tile floor begging for him to call an ambulance. But, he *refused*!

I STARTED OUT life in a very different way; born into sand, sunshine, tropical breezes, and endless summer days surrounded by a clear blue ocean and the scent of tropical flowers wafting through the air: Hawaii.

My mom was fond of saying "I floated in the ocean most of my pregnancy with you." I believe this is partly what imbued the love of the water in my soul. I spent hours snorkeling as ribbons of light shimmered on the sandy sea floor. Peering through my goggles was magical as I floated over colorful fish, eels, and sea turtles while being swayed in the gentle waves, enjoying the freedom and weightlessness of the water.

I was a wild child from the start, running free, partially dressed, into the jungles with no fear. There are many stories told by my parents of their exasperation at finally finding me, only to have me disappear again, away on another adventure.

Most days, I was outside every chance I had, delighting in large patches of monarch butterflies feeding on carefully landscaped marigolds near the entrance to the red mud trails that were my favorite haunts. I was grateful for the freedom that my parents afforded me, allowing my goofy personality, creative outlets, and wildness to thrive.

Little did people know that while they hiked, they were often being watched by a pleasant little forest-dwelling creature, peeking out at them through high tree branches.

Luckily, hanging around our house was almost as fun as the wilderness. My dad, being a near master gardener, terraced behind our cliff house with many cactuses and extraordinary plants. Our garage was far above the house, at the end of an enormous cement staircase surrounded by these gardens. My dad's love of plants and animals led him to build a sizeable outside cage filled with bunnies and guinea pigs, big enough for my sister and me to crawl inside. At night our special Chinese ducks roosted in our trees, safe from neighborhood dogs.

Other than the occasional scolding for eating dry and vaguely meaty biscuits with our poodle out of the dog dish, sticking chopsticks in my dad's tailpipe, or accidentally killing a baby duck when I tried to sit on it as its mommy did, my early years in that bird perch of a house were happy ones.

UNBEKNOWNST TO ME, my parents were drifting apart, as people often do. So, my sister Joanna and I moved, with my mom and a gruff man who later became my stepfather, into a new house on the next mountain over. He believed spanking was a necessary part of discipline, so I disliked and feared that part of him from the very beginning. Usually, there was no need to hit me since I felt terrible just misbehaving, but I stayed away from him as much as possible anyway.

It was at the new house where I met Wilma, one of my best friends. People said she was fat, hairy and dangerous, but I wasn't afraid. Her home was right behind ours; in the backyard precisely. She had been saved as a wee piglet by our landlord after her mother had been killed during a military patrol, and she had grown into a huge, black and brown, curl-tusked boar.

Standing in ankle-deep mud (and probably pig poop), I pet her rough bristles while she ate "pies" I had lovingly made for her (any morsels I scrounged up from the kitchen I thought she would like and my mom wouldn't miss). Many times Wilma chased my sister Joanna and me to a chorus of squeals and screams as we ran across the yard attempting to pick lilikoi (passion fruit) from the vines that laced the fence. The slippery and succulent fruit was worth the risk of a muddy mauling, sitting out of reach high above her, happily eating our drippy orange prizes as she stared up at us, her piggy tail wagging. In the evening we even enjoyed having a little extra dirt, and her slimy snout, dipped into our wooden hot tub as she leaned over the retaining wall while we soaked in the steaming water.

BEING A LITTLE EXPLORER, it wasn't too long before I found, at the very top of a steep hillside where the roads ended, and houses were no longer built, a long hiking trail that became my solace, delight, and a place I longed to return when I was away. The park was called Wa'ahila Ridge, and I hiked for hours up the sharp ridgeline into the clouds, far away from any sights or sounds of civilization. It was just me, the forest, and maybe a Menehune or two (half-naked, elf-like forest creatures who were known to be mischievous).

Native birds sang eerie wistful songs somewhere in the mist that surrounded large Koa and Banyan trees, as breezes softly rattled their leaves. I felt at home climbing on their long damp branches, sitting in nooks under cool misty rains as I snacked on wild tart strawberry guavas and sipped water from their cupped leaves. Rock-wrapped tea leaves occasionally dotted the trails, as an offering of thanks to the area. On later trips, I brought shells and lunches as gifts to share with the mountain spirits and ancestors; leaving a portion nicely wrapped with a leaf tucked into one of my special trees. I always felt loved and welcomed hidden among the drapes of those mountains.

Even with my connection to the forest and trail, the first time I heard "it," I was a bit shaken.

"Na na iki, na na iki," in almost a whisper as if someone had snuck up behind me and jokingly spoken in my ear. With no Internet yet, I headed straight to the library to translate the message. It meant "little observer," and since I enjoyed looking at all the details of the forest, trail, and sky, it was a sweet, poignant, message delivered to me from the spirit world. (Or you could blame it on the Menehunes).

I loved my Hawaiian home where the rocks, trees, and ocean all felt alive to me, and ancient Hawaiian spirits wafted through the forests as I walked slowly on red damp mud and moss trails. However, soon we would be leaving for a smaller and rainier island tucked away on the Northwest Coast of Washington State; Bainbridge Island, the childhood home of my mom. Nervously I packed, said goodbye to Wilma the pig, and cried as I gave my dad a long hug. Then, we drove away from my jungle home.

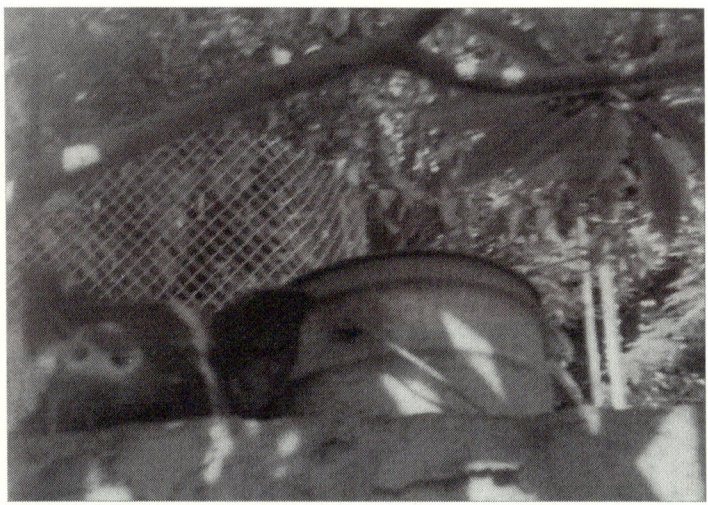

My best friend Wilma the pig.
© *Mom*

When you carry your home
in your heart,
then you can fly.

Mokuna 2: **An Island of Another Kind**

We flew across the ocean. I remember riding in a car headed to my grandparents' beach house. The thick, tall, dark-green fir and pine trees lined the streets, nearly blocking out the sky. We stepped out into their garage to the fragrance of boats, the Puget Sound, and woodworking. My eyes, that appeared turquoise blue in Hawaii, took on a deep olive hue in Washington.

My grandma Pearl had designed the beach house, with the kitchen—as any good German cook would place it—smack dab in the middle of the structure; her needlepoint pillows of Northwest Coast Indian designs, decorated couches, and leather swivel chairs, perched on Asian rugs. A full bank of windows framed the face of the house and looked out to a small yard, just steps away from the seashore and small scurrying crabs. Walking down the rock-and-shell-strewn shoreline made a jolly crunching sound underfoot, as I searched along the delicate lapping interwoven waves for whatever struck my fancy.

A WEATHERED BLUE and white rowboat became one of my favorite toys. After some awkward rowing, oars left crisscrossed and dripping, it was a joy to peer down through kelp and thick swaying horse tail swooshes of seaweed, over the multicolored rocks bejeweled with barnacles while being sloshed back and forth in the playful waves. Flounders' eyes rotated, looking through the water as they hid in the sand. Quick silver fish occasionally darted past, to my excitement. With a dip of my hands, crisp water stinging my skin, one of the bobbing marble-sized jellyfish would be left shimmering in the sunlight and jiggling in my cupped palms until I delicately let it go again.

Inside, the beach house was almost as captivating as the ever-changing shore. Board games abounded and boxes filled with buttons, velvet ribbons, a rainbow of rickrack, and fabric scraps were ever at the ready for a sewing project.

The scrumptious smell of the bottomless cookie jar filled the air, as brightly colored canned jams and fruits lined shelves, and the best homemade pancakes under the sun woke us in the mornings. The happy popping and sizzling of the pancakes were echoed by seagulls chattering away outside.

Still warm and toasty under my grandma's handmade brown, orange and yellow calico quilt, my eyes traced the swirled patterns of the wood ceiling boards as my fingers lazily played with the cheery mandarin orange yarn ties holding the patch-work of colored squares together. But that didn't last long once I heard my grandma call out, "Breakfast is ready!"

Cotton nightie flying, I headed for the sun-bathed breakfast table, hot maple syrup, and orange juice, already being enjoyed by my early-to-rise grandpa and sister Joanna.

If we were extremely lucky she made her cheesecake, the best in the world in my opinion. With my grandmother's silver bob pulled back and a smile on her face, bowls and mixers in a whirl of activity, she smacked away my eager fingers with a wooden spoon every time I tried to grab a taste of the creamy, scrumptious batter. The hardest part was letting the enticing cake cool. I was shooed outside where it was easy to find distractions and entertainment on the endless pebble-strewn beach. As time went on, her cheesecake became my request of choice for almost every special occasion. (If you would like to try her wonderful cheesecake, I have included the recipe in the back of the book).

Another amazing meal she made was her famous clam chowder and homemade bread. During low tides, it was fairly common to see a bucket full of salt water and newly dug clams waiting on the deck, ready for her to make her delicious soup.

IT DIDN'T TAKE LONG until my grandpa Bill offered to take us to Blake Island in his cheery turquoise and white 60's era motor boat buoyed just offshore. Into the rowboat we piled, my sister and I sitting close together on the small paint-chipped back seat as he rowed us closer and closer to the shiny, rocking, boat. As we approached, I was excited and scared all at the same time, having never been in a speedboat before. All the edges and railings seemed slippery as I tried to climb over the rolling and pitching gunwale, but just before I slipped my grandpa's hands reached out and almost effortlessly guided me safely onto the square blue marine cushions with dusty white piping.

He was so proud and happy starting the roaring engine, throttling up and steering us away from the beach, standing tall in his red plaid wool jacket and khaki pants.

From shore, Blake Island looked small, no more than a low hump filled with trees, but it rose up as if by magic as we sped closer and closer, wind blowing as we tore off through waves whipping past seaweed, jellyfish, and birds taking flight away from our path. Sitting across from my sister in her bell-bottom jeans, watching her red curls blowing, we held tight to silver handles smiling at each other as we sat in our oversized, light orange, sun-bleached life jackets pushed up under our chins.

Soon, the beach appeared before us. Again my grandpa helped us out of the boat. It's funny; I don't remember much about the island, except for being surprised that deer were there and being told that they know how to swim.

What has stayed with me through the years were my grandpa's strong and confident hands, and I didn't realize until later in life how special those little moments were and how I would return the favor of strength and support to him one day.

THINKING I WAS NOW a brave seafarer I called a couple friends to come over for a late night rendezvous. It was a cool and spooky night in October; we rowed out across the inky dark water in front of my grandparent's house. We were amazed to see confetti-sized phosphorescence swirling around and flashing alive with every row. Of course, with a youthful irrational mind, I *had* to jump in so I could be surrounded by the beautiful glow. Very quickly the awe changed into panic, as I clawed my way back into the boat to squeals and laughter from my friends (I thought for sure I was going to be eaten by a large salmon or killer whale!). It took me years to live that down.

THE HOME WE MOVED into was a modest coffee-colored clapboard house across the island from my grandparents. It was next to wetlands and a large shallow bay that emptied out during slack tides, allowing for sandy, muddy exploring.

The long dirt driveway was framed by a field of cattails. Red-winged blackbirds hung and spun around the reeds, calling out their odd but mirthful songs.

Our yard was at least twice the size of the house, and if you could brave the enormous banana slugs, pungent skunk weed, sucking mud, thorny vines, and stained fingertips, a romp through the wetlands was rewarded by a handful of blackberries. We were lucky that apple and cherry trees were already growing next to the hundred foot firs that encircled our property, and their fruit could be turned into amazing hot and fresh pies by my mom's expert hands.

During the fall and winter rains, my long narrow basement bedroom often flooded, along with neighborhood yards, which were perfect for slogging around in with rain gear that was useless for keeping us dry as we inevitably splashed and rolled around in the enormous mud puddles, *or* ponds I should say. During storms that often caused power outages, waves dramatically thrashed and crashed over the streets as we watched out through our large, sea-wind-rattled picture window surrounded by candlelight.

The rain and blustery wind storms inevitably gave way to the warmth of summer, with it, the malodorous seaweed smells wafting up from the shore, as we swung on our little old rusty swing set in the backyard. It creaked and cracked, threatening to fall apart with our ever-growing bodies. With just a few minutes' walk, we would arrive at the driftwood-laden shore, and the ever-expanding and retreating tide flats called Manitou beach.

I loved it, like I loved the stinky pink ornate plum tree that smelled like tacos in the springtime, which was edged by enormous rhododendron bushes overburdened by their heavy pompom blossoms in our yard.

Despite my initial sorrow at leaving Hawaii and my dad, as the years went by I came to appreciate both places. We spent summers in Hawaii and the school year in Washington, where I gained some of my best friends, a horse, and one of the sweetest childhood dogs a girl could have wished for.

My black lab mix came into my life one day, offered to me by our neighbors, the family of a soft-spoken, lanky, young man with a shy demeanor, who would later play the bass guitar for a famous Seattle rock band. I remember him telling me that he wanted a quiet, small house somewhere and a horse to ride to town on; and appreciating our family for treating him like himself and not changing because of his career. But I have to admit to being slightly overwhelmed when one day I was hanging out with his mom; an easy going, quick-to-laugh woman with fluffy graying hair who always offered me tea.

It was just the two of us in their fir and cedar tree-embraced shingled house, sipping from our cups and chit-chatting about this and that, when all of a sudden the lead singer with his wild, dark, curly hair—and I assumed the rest of the band—came bounding in, full of energy, talking and carrying on. They were all very nice, but being suddenly surrounded by an influx of male energy was a bit startling. So, I politely thanked her and excused myself, walking out past where eventually a framed gold record would proudly hang, in stark contrast to the simple rustic wall. Then, I grabbed the metal doorknob on their worn wooden front door, turned it, and headed back out into the dappled sunlight and past the very spot where years before I had first seen a beautiful shiny black female dog who needed a home. They explained that they had, "literally saved her from the gas chamber," and asked if I could take her.

I couldn't have been more ecstatic or more grateful for them asking me if I wanted her. And thank God they did, because we were inseparable from the beginning, running on trails, walking on the beach, cuddling during cold, damp, nights. A wheat mark on her chest became a special symbol to me. Her name was Babe, and she became a large part of the early love and joy in my life with the animal world. When my stepfather's emotional trauma reared its ugly head through flashbacks, unpredictable snaps of anger, and reeking sorrow, I rebounded to her overflowing love and comfort.

He recounted his terrifying experiences as a point man in the Vietnam War. This position in a platoon had one of the shortest life expectancies, and no one else in his regiment wanted to go into the dangerous booby-trapped tunnels. He said he survived by developing an almost sixth sense as he crawled deep into dark narrow tunnels as sweat poured down his face and angry red ants did headstands on his exposed skin, sending searing pains into his body as he was gnawed on relentlessly. But he couldn't move quickly or scream out for fear of being found and killed.

I made the mistake of seeing the movie *Platoon* (a graphic movie about the Vietnam War) with him in our local small town theater. With every grimace, groan, jump and disturbed shift in his seat at the horrific images on the screen, my understanding of what he went through and my forgiveness for his outbursts grew.

Luckily, his early years growing up in Hawaii were much kinder to him, all except for one occasion. He loved to tell the story of his and a college buddy's archaeological trip to a Heiau (sacred place of worship for native Hawaiians). He swears he did not take a sacred lava rock, one just "ended up" in his pocket. The curse says that any visitor who takes rocks or sand away from a sacred site will suffer bad luck until the native Hawaiian elements are returned. Well, this site was very remote and only accessible by helicopter, so it was too late to return the rock once he had found it in his pocket.

Several nights later, he was startled awake by Hawaiian night marchers (ghosts of ancient Hawaiian warriors) standing at the foot of his bed.

Leaning towards him in the dim half-light they demanded, "*Take* the rock back!"

After many nights of these intense visitations, he contacted a friend who knew of a local Kahuna (Hawaiian shaman). This man lived in a small shack with no phone or electricity deep in a lush valley near Waimanalo. As they drove up to his house and having never met, they were startled to be greeted by a sinewy, stern, elderly man standing on a small weathered front porch.

The first words out of his mouth were, "*Put* the rock back!"

After explaining they did not have access back to the Heiau site, the shaman reluctantly took the rock, performed a ceremony, and hid it in a place of honor somewhere in his yard.

The night marchers never visited my stepfather again. Unfortunately, the nightmares and memories of Vietnam did.

However enchanting and delightful the rest of my life was in the Northwest, I longed for a respite from the rain and the stresses of our home life. When the end of the school year rolled around, I flew out again across the Pacific Ocean in eager anticipation of adventures with my dad during the long summers in Hawaii.

Babe dog.

Me, and my favorite plum tree that smelled like tacos.

Dive in the ocean,
play in the sunshine,
hide in the wilderness.

Mokuna 3: **Adventures in Paradise**

I t's before the crack of dawn, and no reasonable person is awake at this hour, but we are getting ready for an adventure. A quick stop for doughnuts and coffee, and we are off to the small interisland airport. Swimsuits, shorts, and tabis already on; we're packing light and carrying whatever fits into our dry bags.

After landing on Kaua'i, they threw us kids in the back of an open truck bed on top of all the bags and boats for the hour-long drive to the end of the road.

Destination: Ke'e beach.

At the ripe old age of eleven, I was headed out for my first trip along the Napali coast with my intrepid dad, sister, and a handful of other adventurous souls from the kayak club. Our very first weeklong kayak trip for these wide-eyed adults and kids was spent in single-hulled, flimsy, bright yellow, rubber ducky, 99 dollar kayaks. We stuffed our gear into dry bags and bungee-corded or tied them to whatever strap or loop we could find.

Excitement grew as we started pumping up the boats with foot pumps, slathering on sunscreen, and getting ready to head off down the coast. It was imperative to get to the final beach landing several hours away along the rugged coastline before the winds and waves picked up in the afternoon, making the going rough and dangerous. Of course, our food was accidentally put on a later flight by the airlines, so it was with some urgency that we set off late that morning.

The first task was launching out between the oncoming waves and sharp reefs encircling the beach. Once clear of the dangers and out along the coast, the waves came from the ocean, hit the sea cliff walls, and bounced back, causing washing machine-type waves that spun and bopped us around. Without rudders, we were spinning in circles like the balloons we were. We eventually got used to just "going with the flow" as it were and paddled forward for a while, then backwards, just enjoying the view of the coast, the other paddlers, and the birds in the cliffs. My arms ached on one side, as my dad dug his kayak paddle into the other side trying to keep ourselves headed to our destination.

Eventually, we, and our band of merry (or maybe weary and delirious kayakers) fell into a rhythm as my goofy dad started whistling and singing many tunes. He'd often change the words to suit his jovial personality:

> "My body lies over the ocean; my body lies over the sea; *oh!* My body lies over the ocean; please bring back my body to me!"

The waves splooshed to the rhythm of the songs like a metronome ticking to classical music, as little gray seabirds flew past our heads in punctuation.

Many hours and sore muscles later, there it was; the biggest and scariest beach landing I had ever seen. Even in a kayak with my dad, this would be a tricky landing. Timing was everything. We watched behind us, trying to anticipate the smallest set of waves. Landing on the smallest wave is the ideal of course, but right on its heel is usually a large hulking wave, ready to flip you.

We were as ready as we were ever going to be, so my dad yelled, "Paddle paddle paddle!"

We went as fast and hard as we could, but it was too late. A hulking wave reared up behind us and flipped our flapjack kayak. I was underwater in an instant, rolling around uncontrollably, and remember opening my eyes and seeing only bright yellow as the waves held me under shoving sand into every nook and cranny of my bathing suit.

My dad said he ran to the kayak and, throwing it off of me, saw my eyes huge with fear. Before he could utter the words "Get up the beach!" I was already on the warm sand far from the menacing waves, which was humorous to him. I was not as pleased.

After that, the beach closed out, all landings were basically rolls and crashes. One man's kayak was folded in half in a large wave. Then, it suddenly sprang open again, launching him like an amateur clown shooting from a cannon—minus the crash helmet and garish cape that is—and I may have even heard a yelp as he flew through the salty air just before his impact on the water-logged, frothing sand. Almost all the camping gear he had packed was ripped from the kayak; his army bag torn open, food, clothing, and personal items spinning down the beach. Looking like seagulls swooping in on their latest treats, we grabbed as much as we could for him.

After everyone else landed, we surveyed the scene. We had the entire Kalalau beach and valley pretty much to ourselves, save a few hippies and nudists communing with this amazing and remote place.

Beach caves made the perfect camping site. We fit our entire kayak group in one cave. For beds, some of us used our half-deflated kayaks, made up with slightly damp and sandy sheets, while others made do with sleeping pads on the sand.

At night, dragging the kayaks out to the beach to stare up at the night sky was a popular pastime of ours. I fell asleep beneath shooting stars to the sound of waves in the warm Hawaiian breeze, only to wake in the early morning dew, chilled to the bone. Half-asleep and wrapped in my sheet, I dragged the kayak back into the warmth and shelter of our cave.

The smell of coffee and huge pancakes covered with sunflower seeds worked perfectly to wake us.

My dad's kayak partner and make-shift chef, who was a burly, bearded, redhead from South Africa, covered with freckles, hunkered over the small hissing camp stove handing out his plate-sized masterpieces. "One each," was the rule.

We ate quickly, eagerly anticipating the day ahead, full of hikes, cave swimming, and waterfalls.

As we walked along the beach, my sister and I, to our surprise, saw our first naked people and giggled as they strutted past with burnt boobs and buns where the sun usually did not shine. We met the local resident hippy named Bobo. Trailing along behind, was her "pet" wild baby goat, kicking up its heels and happily jumping on and off of big rocks. Bobo was tall, lean, tan, and friendly.

"All she wore was a smile," my dad loved to say.

She and a group of other naked people formed a pyramid, at my dad's urging, of course, butt side to the camera. He called the "piece" Moons Over Kalalau, and displayed the photo proudly for years. I would love to get my hands on that photo now.

Showering in Kalalau is a splendid experience. The waterfall is right around the corner from the caves and flows delicately into the sand. The falls flow over a twenty-foot smooth rock face, which was perfect to lean back on, letting the brisk refreshing water rinse away the crusty salt and stuck-on sand from our bodies. Several large round gray rocks near the "entrance" block most of the view, and are convenient for setting clothes and towels on. Luckily the pools above the shower were too high and sheltered for any would-be bathers, so there was no worry about any yellow rain.

The caves we slept in were winter wave-battered open lava tubes. There are still narrow, dark, cool and comforting tubes ready to explore, if you keep your hands above your face in the subdued light, protecting your head from hitting low rock ceilings. I found my prized tube half-filled with sand, and crawled back into the elongated cavern enjoying the fragrant mix of salty air and aromatic damp rocks while listening to the occasional tinkling sound of water droplets hitting a shallow pool of standing water near the back of the cave. Leaning against a wall hidden from the world and listening to the muffled surf rolling along the beach outside was so comforting to me as if there was a large heartbeat vibrating from the Earth.

Another adored spot, I found during a lone hike. Everyone was still up at the slip-and-slide falls, which is exactly what it sounds like. Besides a few bruises on your bum, the natural rock slide was a fun destination and satisfying to jump in after a long hot hike. On my way back from the larger falls, I came upon a small pool with no one else around. I found there was just enough room behind the curtain of water to sit on a bit of rock ledge and be completely hidden from view. The white ginger flower I had with me smelled divine as I hunkered behind the delightful pounding veil of water until I was a bit too chilled to enjoy the experience. Refreshed and satisfied, I headed back to the beach and our home away from home.

On a day hike up the long lush valley, my dad nicknamed one of our fellow kayakers "nickel pickle" since besides his wild sun-bleached blond curls, light fuzzy leg hairs, and ample mustache, he wore only a hat, backpack, socks, and hiking boots, carrying his all-important walking stick of course, but was otherwise totally nude. He hiked with all of us clothed people, free as a bird.

Years later and several inches taller, we were back in Kalalau again. I headed out happily, jumping and skipping over the rocks of the recently fallen arch (featured in an early King Kong movie) on our way to swim in large water-filled caves. I was jumping and moving quickly over the newly fallen rocks as I often did without realizing how loose they were, having not been weathered and settled into the sand yet. Jumping off with my right foot, the rock rolled, causing me to land hard on a razor's edge of lava rock. The rock edge was so sharp that it peeled an egg-sized patch of flesh down the front of my left knee. The wound barely bled, just a drop on one edge next to a chunk of fat. I could see one vein going one way and another intersecting it, pulsing as the blood pumped through them. Needlessly to say, I was helped back to camp.

There were two nurses on the trip: "Let's suture it shut," one said casually; "No, I think we should cauterize the wound," said the other.

But I wasn't having any of it. There were few ways out of the remote valley, either a two-day hike or a helicopter ride. Neither was an option, so my dad put hydrogen peroxide on it, wrapped my knee, and proceeded to call me "hop-along catastrophe" as I carried on straight-legged walking around the beach. I did not want to leave the trip and probably couldn't have anyway.

I don't know what inspired me, but I found a small piece of cut bamboo and felt compelled to put little items in it as a healing tool. First I found a pretty red feather on a rock. Red feathers are rare and historically were used by the Hawaiian royalty for decoration. A shell came next, and some bitter leaf. I sat and "inhaled" its light, shifting it to my knee in my mind. That night when a bunch of us were at the beach flopped on our kayaks watching stars, I was doing this and felt like "throwing" the light to my dad. Surprisingly, I could see a glow around him for a few moments in the twilight before fading away. I did this a few more times to make sure I was not imagining it, and there it was. Maybe I wasn't so crazy after all for making a healing contraption.

At night, I dreamt that a beautiful dainty purple-and-green-leafed flower grew out of my knee, the roots pushing up and out the sand that was still in my wound, then the flower turned to crystal and fell off.

Another night, my dreams were filled with small, white-speckled beach crabs wearing green surgeon's masks on their little faces while they stitched up my knee. I appreciated the fun and caring dreams on the coast.

We eventually continued to the next beach, paddling with my leg sticking out of the inflatable kayak and my dad singing and whistling as we went.

Our next stop was Milolii (Me-lo-lee-ee), an expansive coral reef-encircled fisherman's camp with the tiniest mice I had ever seen and large white Pueo (Hawaiian owls) that flew silently through the spooky twilight, flashing their wings briefly between tree branches and moonbeams.

But first, we had a stop to make.

It had been blasted open eons ago by the volcanic eruptions that made Kaua'i, leaving an open ceiling lava tube cave, with a narrow tunnel entrance conveniently pounded open by countless waves and storms over the years. If you were really brave and had the tide and seas with you, one could enter ever so carefully into the inner chamber.

With little steering and even less control, we were going in, past nesting brown noddies swooping closely past our heads and rapidly chirping at our approach. A small waterfall draping one side of the opening offered a refreshing mist on our hot and salty faces.

Once we were committed there was no turning back. Waves came from the ocean swelling into mounds of transparent turquoise-and-aqua-blue water squeezing all of a sudden through the narrow tunnel, one moment lifting us up startlingly quickly, then just as suddenly departing, threatening to slam our boat and bodies into the all-too-close rock walls. Our raised voices were barely audible over the reverberating, thundering sound of the waves as we tried to coordinate our actions, inching and fighting our way until we could breathe a sigh of relief as we entered the almost perfectly cylindrical inner tube that was surprisingly calm and sheltered inside.

It was exhilarating looking up into the crystal blue sky above and glassy deep water that sunk far below us as we waited for the others to attempt their entrances, encouraging them along, as we snacked on crispy peanut butter granola bars and drank orange Tang that covered the taste of the iodine water purification tablets in our waterfall-filled square saline bottles which my dad had proudly recycled from a local hospital.

When we were out and on our way again—as if the caves, waterfalls, and many other sights weren't wonderful enough— a pod of shiny, gray, spinner dolphins flashed and shot out of the ocean with perpetual smiles on their faces and tiny adorable babies keeping perfect time, almost velcroed to their mom's sides. After the main pod swam past and under our kayaks, one dolphin dramatically jumped up so close to the front of our bow I thought the graceful creature might end up in my lap, only to have it dive right in front of us with a great big splash. The ecstatic passing of these dolphins was only eclipsed by humorous and goofy teenager dolphins taking up the rear, by spinning as high as they could, slapping the water, and one did a crooked half jump spin and splat of its own design we thought was most amusing.

The last day had arrived and after our final landing on Polihale State Park beach was completed, there was one more challenge to go. We had to haul our heavy gear-laden kayak over the seemingly endless beach through deep sand as wind sandblasted our legs and oppressive heat stung our already burnt, salt-encrusted skin. I took the front. Slowly we trudged, muscles straining, hands and arms aching.

Halfway up the beach, I was almost ready to give up when my dad called out from behind me in some indeterminate foreign accent he had made up, *"Don't give up, pain* is good for you, makes you strong like *bull!"* (A slightly annoying saying I had heard most of my life that always made me laugh), but he was right, and the cold drinks and fresh pizza smothered with molten cheese waiting for us when we were done weren't bad either.

There was no way we could have known as we teased each other that day how right he would become, but, after 'it' happened he never teased me that way again.

Weeks after we arrived home, and without stitches, my knee finally healed on-its-own. Little pieces of the black and gray sandy bits came out every once in a while, and it still looks like I have some in the ragged, mountain-shaped scar on my knee. But I don't mind; I like to think that I carry around a little bit of Kaua'i with me everywhere I go.

What is under us?

Did you see that shadow there?

Big, white, sharp, shiny, teeth.

*Adventure dad, my stepmom, and me paddling off of
Lanikai.*

© *Photographer, Douglas Peebles*

Mokuna 4: **Harrowing Leaps and Crazy Kayakers**

Every summer, my "adventure dad" and I kayaked as much as possible. He is a proud member of the Hui Wa'a Kaukahi Kayak Club. The club members often came up with *some* crazy day long adventure to entertain themselves, like a good ol' "Weed out the Wimps" paddle.

Their slogan was something like, "*If it ain't blowin', we ain't goin'!*"

Some of them have been known to go out during small craft warnings (when winds have, or are expected to reach, a speed marginally less than gale force). So, of course, I agreed to go, like a fool. With a cotton ball shoved in one ear, due to an ear infection, I spilled into our double kayak.

Ever enthusiastic and unafraid to die, my dad declared, "Ah, you can do it, you are strong, *don't* be a pantie."

The paddle went from Sea Life Park, just before Maka Pu'u (a local surf beach), all the way around past the lighthouse and through multiple wave breaks outside Sandy's (another surf beach). Then, we made our way past the blowhole, and on towards Hanauma Bay, until we finally reached Hawaii Kai's calmer waters to land. The whole trip was six point one miles by car, but feels a heck of a lot longer in a little boat.

The intimidating, deep, dark blue ocean was rough but tolerable as we passed the sharp lighthouse rocks. Then we had to carefully maneuver between two parallel rows of swells continuing along the coast. As you may know, you typically want to keep waves perpendicular to a boat, but during this stretch, the waves came at us sideways threatening to roll us constantly.

Then, we entered the blowhole zone.

Waves and swells grew with each mile. The ocean dwarfed us in our plastic double kayak. Luckily, we were equipped with knee straps to hold us in as wave after wave came upon us. One was so enormous that we started sliding down the back of the wave instead of breaching the crest and smashing down the face. We could hear the next big one coming behind us, roaring and cresting every few minutes, announcing its sinister approach. When it hit, the wave break felt like a giant flushing toilet, trying to rip us off of the kayak. I gripped with my strapped-in legs, trying to keep my okole (butt) in the boat, and luckily we weren't torn, limbs flailing, into the raging seas.

Finally, there was a respite outside of Hanauma Bay. We both jumped in to "make shi shi" as we say in Hawaii, and I told my dad of seeing turtles and hearing distant underwater clicks and whale calls on earlier bathroom stops. So, he proceeded to tell me that the last time he peed here he saw a tiger shark come up to his kayak, look at him, and then descend again. He was quite impressed with the animal. *Crazy man*! Needless to say, I was not as impressed, so I got back into our kayak pronto. Even a mermaid, knows better than to tangle with a tiger shark.

NEXT ON THE AGENDA was a much anticipated outer island, remote-coastline, kayak and camping trip.

"Sharks don't attack inflatable kayaks," they said.

Such was not the case, we found out, in the waters off of one of my favorite islands, and a place that holds a special piece of my heart, where you can still feel a strong presence of old Hawaii. It is wild and rugged with most of the long and skinny island stretched out under dry savanna grasslands. We were headed to the hidden remote north shore where the mountains shot up like cathedrals into the sky, revealing the highest sea cliffs in the world with waterfalls that appeared to fall right out of the sky through the clouds.

My sense of elation grew and I felt like I was going to go see an old friend as we readied our gear, and pumped up our boats with squeaky pumps. We searched the beach for the perfect launching spot to head out around the jutted black rocks, wrapped with foamy white breaking waves, to the back doorway of Moloka'i.

They were an odd pair, to begin with; she a newcomer and he, a man in his seventies. Even though he was strong, they fell far behind the group as she became sicker and sicker, vomiting over the edge of the kayak. Now, when sharks come up to small fishing boats chumming the water, they scrape their open maws along the wooden hulls, trying to get all the tasty morsels. So, of course, a huge tiger shark came up out of the depths, started to scrape the side of their inflatable kayak, and popped it. To their horror, they fell in the water on top of the shark.

The first one on the scene was a photographer. He decided to take pictures of their plight before helping them, so it was my dad and me to the rescue. Luckily, they were fine—startled, but in one piece. We thought the shark was probably just as scared as they were, getting a blast of air in its face just for trying to get a snack. The kayak had a two-foot long gash in the side hull.

My optimistic dad took one look at the gaping hole and said, "Of *course* I can patch it."

Up to his elbows and eyebrows in glue and spare plastic hull patches, he set about mending the huge hole. After which, he drew large shark jaws around the glorious patch job, and wrote in imposing black letters, "SHARK BAIT," on the side.

No one wanted the kayak since it must be "bad luck" and attracts sharks. So, of course, my friend and I (being the tag-a-long, free-ride, little helpers) got "SHARK BAIT."

A couple of days later as we set out to the next campsite miles down the coastline, our kayak slowly deflated with every paddle stroke. We spun around in circles and spent literally hours paddling as hard as we could on one side trying to keep our bow heading the same direction down the coastline. We were so delirious that before long we started singing Beach Boys' songs at the top of our lungs with glee. Even the rear kayaker, meant to keep the group together, left us at last, tired of waiting for the slowest boat to China. We arrived so late we had to eat in the dark. A piece of fat from my boil-in-the-bag camping dinner dropped off my plate and splattered on my friend's foot, making us laugh since we were still as loopy as the sea we just came from.

While eating, we started to hear far off and barely audible cries for help. Not knowing if all our mental faculties were intact, we stopped to listen; still, silent, hearts pounding.

There it was again!

"Help, *Heelllpp!*"

No one else in camp seemed to hear them. The calls became more desperate, and luckily my dad and others believed us, grabbed flashlights and ran up the dark winding switchback trail. The two men were found perched on a cliff edge with no way to navigate their way back to our campsite. Surprise; it was the photographer who had not wanted to leave since he was getting such great sunset pictures.

Even with a hungry tiger shark and a wayward photographer, we were having a wonderful trip. Further down the coastline and after hours of sun-baked, salty, sore-muscle paddling, we rounded a corner and saw giant sphinx-shaped arms of black lava rock covered with soft green foliage, framing turquoise blue water and creating a protected bay with a gentle beach landing.

Our hard-won arrival was rewarded by the best tasting water I have ever had the pleasure to drink. It flowed, naturally chilled and filtered, by layers of lava rock into a tall, narrow, ragged black cave. The small continuous stream made a tiny basin in the wall, just deep enough for us to dip a tin cup in to fill our bottles and parched bodies.

The valley still felt wild and connected to its Hawaiian past. As we hiked further into the interior of the forest, we could almost feel the ancient presence watching us from behind branches and wind-rattled Ti leaves. The ghostly ancestors gave us the impression of being simultaneously loving and kind, while also watchful and protective of the sacred land we were walking on. We came upon an old Hawaiian home site with a huge "family rock" in the entryway, below an expansive shade tree. Three handmade, square, rock bowls complete with small juice channels still sat in a row. Stopping for a snack, we picked delicious mangoes nearby, and I could imagine women pounding the fruit into juice as they chatted and laughed with each other.

Hours later, hot, muddy, and mosquito-bitten, we started our return walk along the river to the beach. I decided it was much more fun—and a mighty bit cooler—to float the shallow, rocky, river back to camp. I was right, and had the stretched-out bathing suit and bruised tush to prove it. I delighted in grabbing fresh guavas along the way, smearing and dripping the pink juices on my face and chest, which I easily washed off by flipping over in the water like a seal as I bobbed along.

At the end of our trip, we were picked up on a rocky, elbow-nook of a beach by a kind and energetic man stricken with leprosy. He had melted facial features, one arm, and a monkey in his old rusty beach-worn, but very helpful, truck. It took several trips to transport us all, as we precariously held onto sun-bleached blue fishing nets and ochre floats, strung loosely on his makeshift wooden truck rack. We tried not to fall out since we were piled high with gear and people as we all bounced along a deeply rutted red road to the small airstrip on Kalaupapa (Ka-laow-pa-pa), the leper colony.

I tried to clean up the best I could before heading back to civilization. On top of a dress-sized blue shirt with my dad's bar logo on it, I tied a piece of white rope around my waist as a make-shift belt (complete with a frayed edge) and dusted the sand from my flip flops. Everyone tried to look presentable, but the dirty clothes, sunburns, and dusty faces, clearly showed the remnants of the remote coastline we had just paddled down. We all helped to load-up the luggage compartments in the wings of the small green and white Air Molokai double prop airplane.

It was time to leave.

As we climbed the stairs to board our flight, I turned around just in time to see a huge, bright, glowing rainbow arching over from the ocean into the mountains, framing the coastline we had just come from. It appeared to our elated group to be a big aloha from the island.

We all stopped to see the brilliant rainbow and call out loud "oos" and "ahhhs" in response. Then I hurried onto the plane so I could be the lucky one to sit up with the pilot like a pretend co-pilot, with the best views of the ship-peppered ocean, occasional whale spouts, and a front row seat through billowing white clouds on our way back to O'ahu.

THE NEXT SUMMER, because things like the "Weed out the Wimps" paddles, and kayaking remote coastlines, seemed too scary, I decided to go skydiving instead.

The balmy day was my nineteenth birthday, and I was taller and heavier than the tiny man that I would be strapped to (who was maybe 5'4 with Prince's boots on). There was one parachute for both of us. But he had jumped over two thousand times, so who was I to question.

I was given a pink hat and eye protection that was too small for me, so I looked like a strange, goggle-eyed, cone-headed freak.

My dad, stepmom, and sister stood by nervously as we watched the disclaimer video with a hairy, bearded, wild-eyed man on the screen who stared out at us ominously, and said, "There is no perfect plane, there is no perfect parachute, no perfect man," then *bam*! All the power shut off, leaving us sitting in the dark. We laughed at the irony of their generator shutting down at such a poignant moment in the video, but somehow it didn't scare me off.

A funny Brit with a camera strapped to his helmet was filming the entire event.

"Don't pay a bit of attention to me, miss, just have fun, okay?"

I attempted to ignore the camera but it was pretty hard with a huge camcorder-looking device strapped to his helmet and pointed right at me.

The tiny airplane climbed for several minutes while I waited in anticipation.

When they finally opened the door we were about to throw our bodies from, my heart started beating *just* a little faster. He yelled over the propeller noise, "Get used to breathing the one-hundred-and-fifty miles per hour air!" Slowly we climbed out of the door onto the wing braces.

"One, two, *three!*" Then loud rushing wind filled my ears as our bodies flew backwards away from the airplane.

Within several seconds of leaving the plane, I had a near mid-air collision with the Brit which later became a comedic fast-action close-up of my head with a cheese-eating grin and my pointy pink hat.

We plummeted toward Earth; five thousand exhilarating feet in forty-five seconds, before a quick lurch after my guide pulled the cord. All of a sudden, the air stilled all around us and became very quiet as we slowed way down and drifted softly. From that view, it looked like I could have brushed the tops of the trees with my toes.

I was elated, even if the off-color joke told by my guide made me blush.

"Almost as good as sex, don't you agree?"

Not quite a woman of the world yet, and I don't mind admitting just a bit socially awkward, all I did was give a courtesy laugh and try to ignore the comment.

The soft floating was abruptly interrupted by a terribly ungraceful landing as I flopped to my knees and belly with him on top of me. The scene resembled twin turtles attached at birth, desperately trying to find some purchase on the ground while attempting to right ourselves. I was embarrassed, but my family was happy I was alive.

BESIDES THE HEART-PUMPING adrenaline, near misses, and joyful delirium that visits to Hawaii came with; another fantastic benefit was the number of far-flung friends and relatives who wanted to visit my dad and stepmom. And I was happy to help them entertain the visitors.

She came from a far away, cold place, with long dark winters. Her home was in the land of the Vikings, and her last name *literally* translated into "The son of Thor." We arrived at the airport, eager to meet our next guest. She was the daughter of a Swedish exchange student my stepmom went to college with. When she stepped out of the airport doors, she was exactly what you would expect—lanky, blond, and friendly. My stepmom and I, up on cheery tip-toes, put fragrant, welcoming leis around her neck, and stuffed her suitcase into the trunk.

During the days ahead, we did as any good "puka shell tour guides" would do and showed her all the best spots around O'ahu.

Sunbathing was also a must, and our time on the beach was not only fun but educational. The very first culturally significant and important words and sayings she taught me in Swedish were: inflatable mattress, bra, thank you for the Swedish language, and Jack in the Box. Add a few jokes (that I am choosing not to share) about her rivals the Norwegians, and I was a full-fledged cultural attaché.

But, she hadn't come this far just to sit on the beach. She wanted to learn to scuba dive, and I was, of course, a very willing partner. We thought learning to dive would be exciting, fun, and dangerous. Expecting to be thrown right in the ocean, we arrived on the first day of class, but we saw chairs and books. After all the pre-requisite studying, tests, and diving gear practice, we were ready! Well, not so fast. First we had to learn to scuba dive in a small, run-down, rectangular pool in Waikiki. We laughed at each other in the echoing pool-house as we tried to stuff our bodies into used wetsuits that were way too tight. Many days and practice dives later, we piled into the dive vans, with the other dive students, and headed out to the leeward coast of O'ahu.

The graduation dive was fabulous. I loved kneeling on the seafloor forty feet down while fish swirled and schooled around our heads. The sea life seemed calmer than the skittish behavior they exhibited when they are hovered over by a snorkeler. I was part of the ocean, no longer an observer peering down from a balcony. My ears never did clear very well, so diving did not become a large part of my life. But luckily, I can still spend hours floating around with a partially-fogged mask, and a snorkel shoved in my mouth, just happy as a clam; watching fish, turtles, and stingrays appear out of the depths in front of me. Nowadays, I try to move more gently through the water, flowing in and around the coral with the waves, so I am just a *little* less scary.

At the end of "the daughter of Vikings" visit, we were both equipped with golden tans, sun-bleached hair, and brand new, shiny, diving certificates. We boarded our planes and flew away to very different parts of the world. I hope one day to visit her in Sweden. And with my extensive Swedish vocabulary, at least I will be able to buy a bra if I forget to pack mine in the suitcase.

Diving was great, but a large, robust, and beefy friend was anxiously awaiting my return to Washington. And I had been away from her for far too long.

Here is the "daughter of Vikings," taken on a vintage camera.

© C.M. Arvish

A horse is both a friend,
and freedom.

Mokuna 5: A **Horse of Course**

What little girl *doesn't* want a horse? My horse came about when, one afternoon, a friend and I stepped out of a woodland trail and were charged by several girls on horseback. Three brutish girls, astride large imposing beasts, trotted quickly toward us from an adjoining small country road. We had been chatting happily, unaware of the approaching danger as we walked along our frequented trail. It wove its way through the many houses in our neighborhood—a classic child's short cut.

We must have looked like perfect targets. So, laughing and delighted with themselves, the girls steered their horses straight at us, as if to play a game of "chicken." Unfortunately, the trail was so small they pushed us aside aggressively. Shocked, but mostly fine, we dusted ourselves off while yelling our displeasure at them. We were basically unscathed, except for one of my feet, now swelling and in pain after being stepped on when I tried to face down one of the horse and riders. The horse that stomped on my foot that day later became my chestnut mare. I had no idea, as I was nursing my sore and bruised foot, I would end up owning and loving her for fourteen years.

My stepfather was the one that met her rider on the beach. Being thoughtful, he set it up for me to take care of Castaña (Cas-tanya) while her owner went away to college in Spain. The first time I excitedly approached Castaña's pasture and met her owner, I recognized them right away, but never mentioned anything. Neither Castaña nor her owner appeared brutish or imposing that day, in fact both were delightful.

She was a Spanish Barb (Spanish Arabian mixed with a hearty North African breed). Her long face and sturdy build were common characteristics of the mix. They had shipped her from Spain with them when they moved to the United States. After a couple of years of caring for Castaña, I bought her when we were both twelve years old for $200.00 that I had saved up.

I rode her bareback almost the whole time I owned her. She was fourteen-and-a-half hands tall, just over the size of a large pony. I could ask her to stay, and then after backing up, take a running start and jump my belly onto her back while swinging my leg over her. Most of the time it worked; but sometimes she had to patiently wait, curved neck staring back at me, as I re-doubled my efforts.

We occasionally rode on the beach, but once out on the tide flats she turned into a *crazy* horse. She reared and pawed the water before throwing me off her back, charging through leg-breaking logs and running across a two-lane street, back to her pasture. We stopped going out to the flats after that, and once I got her over her fear of semi-trucks, garbage cans, and sheep, she was pretty much bombproof.

We spent years on lush trails riding through the woods, swimming in the water when the tide was in, and meeting up with other girlfriends and their horses. Castaña was truly a good friend and a patient horse. She tolerated being dressed up in costumes for Halloween, wearing clip-on earrings, garter belts, and being decked out in ribbons and Christmas lights for the holiday season, sleigh bells and all. On the coldest days, she even allowed me to warm my cold winter fingers in the hot steaming breath coming from her nostrils.

I remember nights laying backwards on her, almost hugging her large rump, resting my cheek on her hip bones as she grazed in the grass under the stars, almost falling asleep as she swayed back and forth, walking slowly in her pasture.

I did my best as a teenager to take care of her, but there were evenings I forgot to feed her.

Early in the morning, flustered and half asleep, rubbing her eyes, my mom would ask, "Did you feed Castaña last night?" She went on to recount the horrible dream she'd had the night before of Castaña half starved and emaciated.

Trusting my mom's dream, while remembering my foible, I headed out early many brisk mornings, feeling bad, running up to her pasture and giving her alfalfa hay and extra oats right away. She forgave me quickly and was as eager as ever to go for a trail ride on the many backcountry dirt roads and thick wooded trails.

One crisp morning, we were exploring in the woods on an unknown trail which suddenly became steeper and steeper— there was a hill on our left, and a cliff on the right. We had no way to turn around, or to go back. I became frightened and did not know what to do, so I just closed my eyes, held onto her reassuring strands of rough mane, clicked, and asked her to get us out of this. Her sweaty muscles strained beneath me and her lungs heaved loud powerful breaths as branches cracked under her hooves and the ground shifted precariously underneath. Leaves and branches stung as they swatted my face, scratching my cheeks and arms. But still, I held tight, eyes clamped shut, trusting in her strength, wisdom, and her senses that were finely attuned to the natural world. I had to have faith that she knew the way, and sure enough, she trudged and climbed us out of there. I did not open my eyes until I felt her efforts lighten. Extra treats and grain were on the menu when we finally arrived back at her pasture. I am sure she saved us that day.

IN THE SPRINGTIME when the fields were full of grass and she was full of gas, I sang a little song to her as we went along our way.

"Ohhhhh, *she's* my farting horse; she farts to the left, and she farts to the right, she farts all day, and she farts all night, Ohhh *she's* my farting horse."

I 'm sure she really appreciated it.

Also, on the less rainy spring and summer days, Castaña loved to graze leisurely on our half acre plot. Our yard was un-fenced; the only natural barrier was the tributary streaked swamp, woven with brambles at the bottom of our hill. I thought nothing of riding her to our home from her pasture with only a halter and lead rope, then sliding off her back and walking up to our house without a care. I often left her to graze and lounge in our yard, unrestrained. She never left or attempted to flee.

This went on periodically for years. One of her favorite past-times was napping at the foot of our yard between the pine trees and our Curly Willow. Often, with quiet glee, I tried to peek around a tree, or sneak up to her while she slept, only to be thwarted by her keen hearing.

With a groan, she would rise to her hooves quickly, shake out her large body—making a cloud of dirt and hair around her—and nicker softly as she walked towards me in anticipation of the inevitable treat hiding in my pocket.

But *finally,* one warm morning, I had become stealthy enough to approach her unnoticed. It became one of our sweetest moments that I cherish. She slumbered happily in our yard. Barefoot, I quietly crept up to her through the cool damp grass as she slept on her side, dreaming like a dog, eyes and hooves moving. She awoke sleepily and came halfway up, so I sat quietly, trying not to disturb her. She *slowly* lay back down, her huge heavy head resting on my lap. I delicately pet her cheek, careful not to wake her. I loved her soft chestnut colored hair and how she smelled of chewed grass and sunshine. I stayed like that as long as possible, but after a while, my legs ached and started going numb. So, even though I didn't want to move, I eventually got up and left her to enjoy her nap.

IT WAS WITH MUCH reluctance, after fourteen years, that I finally sold my beautiful Castaña. I was living in another state and only came to Washington on occasions; leaving friends and eager neighbors to care for her.

I had visited the week before, only to find the soon-to-be-owner's mom brushing her, getting ready for a ride as if everything was fine. I could see *instantly* that Castaña was in distress. Veins bulged on her face; her head hung low with eyes half closed. She barely wanted to walk. I found the wound right away. Scanning the pasture I saw the culprit; metal tree stakes she must have used to scratch her itchy, bug-bitten teats on. The dirt had given way beneath her weight, and a stake had punctured her udder, leaving a nasty oozing hole.

I held her face while we waited for the veterinarian, her forehead and nose pressed up against my chest and belly, talking softly, trying to comfort her pain.

Fortunately, after some much-needed sanitizing, stitches, pain medication, antibiotics and healing, she was fine, but I was even more uneasy about selling her.

When the day arrived to bring the bill of sale to her new owner's house, I couldn't help sobbing uncontrollably as I signed over my precious horse to them. As I walked away from their house and away from her pasture, my heart shattered into a million pieces and blew away like the dust on the dirt road I was walking on.

She ran to the farthest corner of her fence after me, whinnying frantically, almost sounding like a scream, chest pressed hard against the wooden fence, thrashing her head around, trapped and unable to reach me. I should have run back to her, hugged her neck, told her that I loved her and was sorry, but I just turned my back and walked away. It hurt too much to see her.

I don't know how she knew that day was different from any other, but somehow she knew.

I was only able to visit her a few times in the years after I sold her.

My mom had been banned from seeing her after calling the veterinarian without the owner's consent when she saw how skinny Castaña had become. It was explained to my mom by the angry owners and a befuddled veterinarian that they were told to put her on a diet. My mom said she understood, but still crept up to her pasture, like a ninja under the cover of darkness, and gave her treats whenever she could.

The owner's anger eventually softened, and I felt better when they described the barn they had built for her, the warm blankets she wore in winter, vegetable scraps she was given from their large garden, and the ribbons their daughter had proudly won with her in small home-town horse shows.

Eventually, I felt better about having sold her, knowing she had an ever-mindful ninja mom to keep an eye on her, but I never stopped missing her and hoped she understood why I left. I was very happy to have had her for so long. She was a great gift.

When she was too old to ride, they let her retire. After she died, they buried her on their property, saving three locks of her mane, braided and tied with bows, for her "three girls" (we three who had owned, loved and ridden her throughout her long life). I still have her soft mane, tied with a sheer red bow, hanging on one of my cherished framed pictures of her. The picture shows her standing in a field of yellow buttercups, head held high, with a shiny summer coat, bright white stripe on her face, and her tail flicking sideways.

CASTAÑA ALSO HELPED to usher into my life a goofy, fun, wise, and short best friend. Yep; she is cute as a crumpet, maybe 5'1 in heels on a good day. She liked to stretch up and say that she is "5'1 and a half." My little, half-Spanish, half-Norwegian, Kelsey.

I remember the first time I saw her, shyly walking into gym class cloaked in a big shirt and sweats, her short dark hair partially hiding her face as she looked at the floor, lost and new.

The next period, as she sat behind me in History, I spun around in my chair and enthusiastically introduced myself.

"I have a horse; do you want to meet her?"

That was all it took. I rode over to her house after school and the rest is history. I had always been shy, but her disarming charm and unguarded playfulness removed all of that. She, her five siblings, and their mother had just moved up from California, and as each one came home I was shocked at how similar they all looked. Dark ringlet hair, light brown skin, and pretty.

Her room was all decorated pink. Pink phone, pink high tops, pink chair, pink bedding, and a pink hairbrush. The very first song we listened to together was George Michael's "Father Figure," on her pink boom box.

WE HAD AN instant connection, and enjoyed climbing trees, hiking, fishing, combing beaches, kayaking, crafting, and swimming on seaweed draped logs in our school clothes. Thirty feet from the school bus stop, we'd climb over the driftwood and head straight into the salt water. During rainy downpours, we enjoyed laughing at our idiocy as our limbs turned numb, and we were eventually forced to slog up to my house shivering. It is to my mom's credit that she allowed us to strip in the basement, leaving piles of happy messy clothes, and drain the hot water tank as we thawed out in the shower.

Her siblings were thick with personality and humor. Since I was very gullible, and easy to tease, I never questioned one of her sisters who called me "chocha" for years with a smirk. I thought the nickname was a term of endearment, but finally, she confessed through her laughter that she had been calling me 'lady parts' in Spanish the whole time. We all got a good hoot out of her joke.

Many days after school we piled into their wood-paneled home, hungry and giddy with expectations of the afternoon's exploring, and frivolity. I don't know how their mother fed them (us) all; if there was ice cream or delicious food in the house, it disappeared before you knew it.

Over the years, we enjoyed many adventures together on the mainland. Then, one summer, I was lucky enough to bring Kelsey to Hawaii with me.

Castaña, poses for her picture, in a field of Buttercups.

© *C.M. Arvish*

At least, difficult journeys often lead
to wonderful destinations.

Mokuna 6: **Princess Papouli and A Mid-day Moon**

The kayak club drove us along the Hana highway, curving back and forth in-between waterfalls, over aging moss-patched bridges and past sea cliffs, until we reached the end of the winding road. Once all the kayakers were packed and ready to go; into the water Kelsey and I forged, each carrying one end of our hot pink, hard-shelled, two-person, sit-on-top, Ocean Kayak.

"Ready to go?" I asked as we entered the menacing waves.

As Kelsey began to be battered and bumped around by the surf-slapped kayak, I heard panic mount sharply in her voice. "I can't do this!" She said, "What do I do?!"

We stood chest high in the waves while water splashed our faces and bounced us around, paddle in one hand as we tried to steady ourselves. She was struggling to kick herself on board while being knocked around by the long hard kayak. Even though this was old-hat to me, together we had only paddled in the Puget Sound, in relatively calm waters.

With a startled realization, I was shocked into action—spitting out details and commands like a hippy kayaker drill sergeant.

"Jump in, watch your paddle leash, kick hard, hold tight, keep the nose to the waves, paddle hard!" As we and all our flailing limbs somehow piled onto the boat in one piece.

I had never thought of how different Hawaiian waters were going to be for her, until she started turning gray just minutes out, leaning sideways, eyes half closed, appearing as if she was passing out and almost falling into the turbulent ocean.

"Put on your life vest!" I demanded.

We were in a long double kayak; tough to steer on the best of days with two people, but as she became more and more seasick and weak, it was up to me to handle the entire beast myself, with miles to go until our first beach landing and campsite.

This was scary, but in my dad's brave and nonchalant way, he came up beside us, made sure we were basically ok, and started to sing.

"Princess Papouli got plenty papayas, she *likes* to give them away." (In his mind, she looked like a princess having her royal highness paddled down the coast).

Finally, with a little urging and some more humor, we came within sight of Waianapanapa (why-napa-napa), or as my dad likes to say, "*Why* not Waianapanapa?"

Since there was no way I could steer our whale of a boat into a surf landing, we flopped out into the swells, and I helped Kelsey to the beach, while a beefy male kayaker from our troop landed the kayak for us. I swore I was not trying to kill her, but she teased me just the same.

That evening we hiked and swam in two water caves.

Dad offered to send Kelsey back, but she and I refused! We were going, come what may.

The next day, as we forged down the coastline, the first thing we tried was dragging her behind the kayak, floating her along in a life preserver while she snorkeled. She felt too much like shark bait, so we stopped that experiment. Some nice people from our group offered to swap their single kayaks for our large double. In a single kayak, and dosed with Dramamine, she seemed to fair a bit better.

No one had been on this coastline before our weeklong camping trip, so the next landing was up for interpretation. Brave, nothing-scares-me Dad, wanted to try to land on a long sandy beach, through three sets of waves breaking hard and coming straight from the ocean.

"*No!*" I said, "I don't care if Kelsey and I camp alone," I was not landing on the wave-pounded beach! I pushed on, not looking back, as Dad and the other paddlers laughed and finally relented.

I could see that not too far away, the land stuck out, resembling sphinx's arms. I knew from kayaking down Moloka'i's remote coastline that a sphinx-like formation often hides a protected beach landing.

Once around the corner, calm soothing waters appeared, framed by a couple of small soft beaches parted only by a pristine stream flowing into the ocean. We paddled through the tiny breakers up into the small river, slowed by the gentle water underneath us. Undercut roots arched out from the pinkish gray colored ground, making ideal moorings.

After securing our kayaks, we took a few minutes to indulge in a favorite Hawaiian bathing ritual: using Shampoo Ginger flowers to wash our hair. We found, blooming all along the stream, the perfectly ripe, plump, flaming red flowers. We chose a couple each, and I showed Kelsey how to squeeze the mildly spicy smelling, slippery, natural soap into our hands before washing our hair. We enjoyed lying down in the river and chatting for a bit, but something caught our attention.

Refreshed, and barely unpacked, we stared up into the river valley. It begged for us to explore it.

While waiting for the others to arrive, we took off, following the river into the jungle. If we were lucky, we might find a small waterfall or two. Tabis, water bottles, and granola bars at the ready, we went up alone, leaving the other slow pokes to set up their campsites after us. We climbed over large round lichen-laced rocks, seeing freshwater Opi'i (snails) as we went.

This was the most unspoiled, lush, quiet, and idyllic Hawaiian valley we had ever been in. The smell of the forest and flowers was intoxicating. Ever so slowly, we began to hear a sound like a far-off airplane, then a rumble, louder and louder as we went faster and faster, our excitement growing. Just around the last bend, we saw it: one of the most beautiful roaring falls we had ever seen. It towered at least two stories high, with a clear shimmering pool, multi-colored impatiens, and white Hawaiian ginger flowers encircling the edges.

Eagerly we swam through the pool, closer to the pounding water, climbing hand over foot up soft moss-covered rocks until we sat behind the falls. This was a slice of heaven. Even the little blue prawn, that pinched me as I poked at it in its hole, couldn't dampen my spirits. Again and again, we jumped through the cold rushing water into the deep pool. This was the most amazing waterfall, valley, and beach we had ever had the honor of exploring.

We were having the time of our lives, but knew the others would enjoy this too, so off we scampered, back to the beach, to retrieve our fellow adventurers.

The valley was clean and protected. The kayaker's code is to be careful and respectful while we are having fun and leave no trash or disruption. So, as we all swam and played among the jungle and waterfall; care, respect, and reverence were given to this incredible place we found ourselves.

After a long day, back at the campsite, the whole clan sat on the sand, or their folding camping seats, ready to eat fresh fire-cooked fish caught on a kayaker's long-line and some fresh-water Opi'i, or Hihiwai (like Hawaiian escargot). Kelsey and I plucked some of the little snails from the river and proudly cooked them on the fire, but failed miserably. I nearly vomited when I felt the hot, sticky, snot-like glue of it all stuck to my lips and tongue. I spun around gagging and spitting. Apparently, we forgot to open the operculum (the lid-like structure the snail uses to close the opening of the shell when it's retracted inside) before putting the butter and spices on to cook, so they were almost raw.

As the days passed, we kayak-camped at many beaches along the coastline. Valleys with hidden Hawaiian rock walls and lush green canopies imbued with stinky, decaying fruit and flower smells hanging in the humid air, gave way to a drier, rockier landscape. The waves—to our and especially Kelsey's relief—became smaller and calmer near the end of the trip.

On the last day, our ragtag, sunburnt group landed on the beach in front of our rented condo. Gear went everywhere, spread out on the lawn as we unpacked and hosed off the kayaks. Instead of helping, some felt more like resting in the breezy hammocks. Our salty-dog complexions were revealed to us for the first time in a week and all we could do was laugh as we peered into the bathroom mirror at ourselves. No matter how great a remote coast trip is, sleeping in a "real" bed, eating in a restaurant to our hearts' content, and having a nice hot shower, is a welcome treat.

Years later, Kelsey reminded me with a snicker that as a tourist helicopter flew through the valley and almost on top of our campsite, I had pulled down my shorts and flashed them a full moon in the middle of the day. Somehow I had blocked out that fun tidbit, but I am glad she reminded me.

Back on the mainland, suntans fading again into the Washington weather, we had *so* much more to talk about over the fall and winter, now that she had experienced her *very own* Hawaiian adventure.

Dad, enjoying some kayak fishing off of Maui.
© *Stepmom*

Kelsey and I, before she almost passed out.

© Dad

Angels live all around us.

They might hide their wings
and dart between moonbeams;
but there is no denying the hope
and the peace they bring.

Mokuna 7: **Hippies and Angels**

The small ten-by-five-mile Northwest Coast Island—that I was beginning to call home—was where my mom grew up. Since she was raised in a conservative household, she longed to expand her personal and spiritual horizons. That led the rebel rouser in her to head straight for Hawaii. Now with two children in tow and one on the way, she set her roots firmly back into this little island.

On many days, rain or shine, I was gone all day with my friends on horseback, fishing off of docks, boating, or just beach combing, and she never restrained this. My room was an enormously messy, artsy, eclectic space where I was allowed freedom of expression. The chaos drove my grandma crazy, but I always appreciated being allowed to paint all over the walls and I am sure it is what lead to all the murals I painted later in life.

In Hawaii, my mom was a premier female stained-glass artist, so I spent hours of my childhood watching her create and build windows in her art studio, learning by osmosis. I ended up helping her to build several large and colorful stained-glass windows in churches on Bainbridge Island when I was older. One installation was an engaging and complex

Chagall-style octagonal window set in the ceiling above the baptismal font in St. Cecilia's Church.

We had made a special trip to the grand stained-glass showroom of Cline Glass in Portland, Oregon, searching through the "Saturday Night Specials" for the one-of-a-kind sheets of glass made by eccentric, fiery artists. These pieces would imbue our window with all the colors and textures we needed.

I spotted a piece of baroque glass peeking out from under layers of smaller broken and pre-cut sheets stacked up in a dusty wooden bin. *This looks perfect for the horn of St. Cecilia* (the patroness of musicians), I thought. With the tips of my fingers, trying to avoid cutting myself on the razor-sharp edges, I finally dislodged the triangular gem and held it up to the light. The gold and caramel ripples rose and gleamed like sheer shimmering silk, frozen in space.

Back at my mom's studio, all the sheets of vibrant glass we had bought were wrapped and stacked in preparation for us to choose the perfect angles, colors, and light to shine through the finished window, but one piece sat alone.

Most of the less complex cuts I happily helped with, but we only had one chance for the curved horn. New oil was applied to mom's sharpest cutter. The golden triangle sat in the middle of her large cutting table as she approached.

Looking up at me with anticipation she said, "We only get one shot."

With the rippled side down, her diamond-tipped tiny circle blade made scratching, slightly squeaky noises as she pushed slowly over the glass, curving, inching as she went. Snap! The first piece was done. A few more tense moments . . . snap! Another and another . . . almost done.   The internal curve, if not expertly cut, could shatter the whole piece right across the middle. Alligator snips pliers now munched and crunched out the inside curve, like eating shards of glass watermelon, until every tiny piece was detached, leaving only what we needed. A one-of-a-kind horn fit for a saint. She had done it, and it fit perfectly. I loved working on that commission with her from beginning to installation, and the horn is still my favorite piece in the window.

We had to leave the project incomplete since, sadly, the visionary Priest who hired us died suddenly of a heart attack. I keep the designs safe, and find myself often imagining being able to one day return to the church and fill the windows around the podium with all the colors and light that he had longed for.

Thankfully, I was able to help her build a few more large stained-glass windows for churches and family homes after the "Chagall" piece. Years of lead poisoning from soldering started hurting her joints, so she eventually had to stop, leaving behind many great and vibrant works.

AFTER MOVING BACK to Bainbridge Island my mom started to meet, and learn spiritual ways from, First Nation's people in the area. When we were finally allowed as guests into sweat lodges, I was fascinated by the ceremony and the feeling of spiritual awe that came with it. I was taught to make prayer ties and some of the more intricate rituals surrounding the sacred practice. Later, I was humbled when I was asked to be a rock tender. Our family friend and pipe carrier said I could, "feel the energies," which is a great honor, for a non-native person.

Once I had more experience, I went to Canada and helped build a lodge on a swan rookery. It was a very beautiful site, situated on the edge of a cattail and willow-edged pond, with elegant swans lightly bobbing or quietly honking, while some of their brethren flew past us high above.

I had traveled there with our family friend, who ran many sweat lodges. He was gratified that, with little to no instruction, I could intuitively find the proper willow branches while helping build the lodges 'ribs' with him. I felt proud and special to be involved so intimately with the process.

After evening set and the stones were hot, we all quietly sat deep inside the dark embracing sweat lodge, as a thick layer of blankets and a feeling of sacred power surrounded all of us. Bits of sage and dried cedar crackled on the hot rocks, sending small ribbons of fragrant smoke into the air. Little orange glowing ember eyes from the pit popped and pulsated in the warm enveloping darkness. We took turns praying or sharing whatever was in our hearts or minds, and then respectfully concluded by saying "All my relations."

At times, when the heat and steam became almost unbearable, I cheated, and snuck one of my hands out under the blankets and into the cold damp grass, relishing that small portion of my body having relief. After each round, our reward was emerging into the cool refreshing air and standing on soft ground, our bodies steaming in the moonlight.

Afterward, still damp and sweaty, with dirty bare feet, we shared food, laughs, and a feeling of somehow being lighter after going through such an intimate, personal, and sacred ceremony together.

During those cleansing and powerful experiences, I felt guided, protected, elated, and bonded with many that attended the sweat lodges with me.

IT WAS WITH THAT history and reverence for the ceremony that my mom and I showed up on a cool crisp night, stars shining, ready for another sweat lodge.

All of a sudden, we noticed people laughing as they danced, writhing, partially dressed, to music, rolling over each other in what I can only describe as a "cosmic ecstasy," as they made strange faces and noises. We decided to be "open-minded" and stay. The sweat leader was not native like we were used to, but a tall, sinewy, long-haired, fluffy-mustached, self-ordained guru, who put the pit of rocks right in front of himself instead of in the middle of the lodge. In between the prayer portions, when we crawled or kneeled back out of the lodge, he forcefully pushed us out by our butts and loudly grunted, making obnoxious groans as if we were being birthed from the lodge. It was all we could do not to laugh. My mom and I smiled and giggled under our breaths at each other, trying to be polite. At least making the meditation prayer sticks was fun, but we did not go back there again. Mom was feeling a strong tugging from the spiritual realm, trying to get her attention, shifting her focus.

IT'S WITH HER PERMISSION that I describe to you what happened next.

She felt determined to visit sacred sites in the Southwest.

My mom and a friend of a friend—we will call him Ed, were going to help each other make the drive.

Neither of them had been there before, and it was in the middle of winter, but they *had* to go to the desert, the Hopi mesas to be exact.

They left just days after Christmas on my mom's birthday—come what may.

Their vehicle of choice? My mom's maroon Dodge caravan typically used to shuttle family members and pets around—now called the "road warrior." She and this barely known companion set off into the night.

Driving wind and snow blew sideways across the roadway, nearly blocking out their sight. Soon they arrived at the dreaded mountain pass. All the truckers and most of the cars were parked on the side of the road, unable to continue.

My mom quieted her mind, diving deep into meditative prayers, asking for help and directions for their travels. Then, all of a sudden, and to her surprise, she received a response, but from what source she could not exactly say.

The loving, disembodied voice said, "Park between the trucks, safe and out of the wind, wait there. I will tell you when it is safe to proceed." Content with this message, they tried to find comfort and warmth in the van. While waiting for the storm to pass, they both fell asleep. In the early morning, while it was still dark out, my mom was awoken.

Gently flowing again into her consciousness, the voice said to her, "It is *time* to go."

They complied, and were able to drive safely alone over the pass without incident, thankful for the guidance.

Blazing right through Idaho and Utah with no problems, they felt hopeful for an easy drive the rest of the way to the mesas.

Then, they arrived at Chaco Canyon.

The road was a "slippery snot mud pit." The van struggled to gain ground and traction in the ever-deepening mud and rain. Deciding to stop and wait seemed their best course of action when out of nowhere two very strange looking drunken men approached the van. *But from where?* No one else that they could see was crazy enough to try the drive. The men came close to the van but did not approach any further. Mom and Ed were uncomfortable with the new arrivals and did not know what to do, so, on they forged. Many tense and hair-raising miles later they arrived at the Chaco Culture National Historical Park Center.

Relieved to have arrived in one piece, stretching their weary bodies, they marveled at a sky rippled with dramatic dark clouds, lightning, and rainbows above the terra cotta-colored rock formations.

Distracted by the spectacular scenery, with fresh rain and a light wind blowing sand through the fragrant sage, they didn't notice a very shocked woman approach them from out of the visitor center. "Where in the *world* did you come from? I heard the road was impassable! Please come in out of the cold." They both happily followed.

Mom *knew* they were supposed to see someone on one of the mesas, but it wasn't clear yet who, when or where. In the gift shop, she picked up a book, opened it and the idea for their next destination smacked her in the face. Hotevilla, or the 3rd Mesa as it was known. *That was it*, somehow she instinctively knew 3rd Mesa was where they needed to go. She showed her companion and he heartily agreed, but how to leave? The roads were only getting worse.

Again she prayed for assistance.

And again, something answered her.

"Go ahead and sleep, I will freeze the ground, then let you know when it is safe to leave." Tucking into blankets, trying to be as comfortable as possible, they waited. At precisely 3 o'clock in the morning, she was gently awoken.

"It is *time* to go," said the gentle disembodied voice.

They started to drive, and sure enough, to their amazement, the road had frozen, making their drive out easy and free from obstacles.

THE NEXT DAY, before heading to Hotevilla—like any good tourists—they stopped at 2nd mesa and perused an artist's shop. Their heading was now clear, but who to contact? Only knowing one elder's name, she asked the shopkeeper if by chance she knew the man and where to find him.

"He is away from home most of the time and usually not available," the woman responded, "but there he is right now, across the street, working on his ladder."

She thanked the woman and awkwardly approached him, honestly explaining why she and her companion were there.

With kindness, he offered popcorn, welcoming them inside his earthy but nice concrete block home. Handmade rugs adorned the dirt floors along with simple furnishings, blankets, and a rustic yet comfortable interior.

After a brief visit, he was nice enough to give them the name of an elder to meet on 3rd mesa and directions to his home, and sent them on their way.

Looking up as they were leaving, she saw another woman across the street, which, at a glance, could almost be her doppelganger.

Mom thought, *with my curly, unruly strawberry blonde hair, comfy traveling clothes, fanny pack, and beloved, well-worn Birkenstocks—how in the world is the elder going to recognize me when I look like every other outsider?* The only unique feature of her appearance is one blue and one brown eye hidden beneath her partially purple prescription glasses.

Now, 3rd mesa is very traditional. Most of the residents (especially the elders) refused modern electricity, government piping, sewer, phone lines etcetera. They have kept their community very primitive and have been proud of it for years. As far as my mom and Ed knew, there was no way to warn their impromptu host of their impending arrival.

Tentatively driving up the dirt road, admiring the monochromatic adobe and concrete houses built in amongst rocks and boulders, they were surprised to be greeted by the very person they hoped to meet. "I have waited a long time for you to arrive," he said.

He was a petite man with a big spirit and bright eyes, sporting cropped salt and pepper locks pulled back into a ponytail, with a cotton button-up shirt tucked under a simple brown leather belt and jeans. After warm welcomes, he showed them around the mesa, ending up back at his house built next to a Kiva with a wooden ladder worn smooth, sticking out of the hole in the roof.

The only lighting inside of his home was a copper kerosene lantern hanging above a large wooden table. Gorgeous rugs covered most of the dirt floor. Family items and personal mementos were mixed in with strikingly patterned blankets draping their couch next to an entire wall filled with Kachina dolls in various colorful dress and dancing poses. Wood popped quietly in the large cook stove, keeping their home and tea water warm.

In the kitchen stood the elder's cute wife, in her flower print apron. She quickly insisted, "You need to sit down and listen to him." She served them herbal tea, and then it started.

Like a download of information, the elder began to speak. He told them of the history of the Hopi and of all people. He talked about what was coming—prophecies, petroglyphs, their meanings and sacred teachings.

They were so absorbed in what was being said; they hardly noticed the passage of time. One of the elder's daughters came home, and they may have been served chicken; but mom and Ed were focusing so intently, that what was happening around them faded into the background.

The elder talked for hours, deep into the night. Mom and her companion were transfixed and filled with a new responsibility and honor after being entrusted with such sacred and vital information.

When all was said and done, the elder invited them to stay the night. Then, right on cue, a very strange and obnoxious person showed up. They kindly thanked him with all of their hearts and left.

That night, after they departed, the mesas were cut off to outsiders for an indeterminate amount of time. They felt lucky to have arrived just before the mesas were closed.

I have to admit, out of all of the fascinating and important messages the elder shared with my mom that day, there was one saying I loved the most.

He said, "The world will be saved by people with big hearts."

YEARS LATER MOM LIVED on a reservation near Poulsbo, Washington, helping with community revitalization projects. One of these was getting back very important native lands previously lost to history and connected to Chief Sealth, more commonly known as Chief Seattle. After living near an indigenous population for a while, she said it amazed her that a group of people, having experienced many hardships and at times suffering atrocities, could still find the grace in their hearts to allow outsiders into their intimate circles and share such sacred teachings and knowledge.

She will never boast about her contributions and accomplishments in many areas of her life, but I am proud of her kindness, wisdom, selfless giving and humanity. So, I will toot her horn, just a little.

I ALWAYS ENJOYED listening to my mom and her friends talk about their spiritual adventures, natural wisdoms from around the world, and even some ghost stories that intrigued me. So, when she was introduced to a native teacher, we went to a gathering to hear his stories, filled with life lessons and guidance from the realm beyond.

The gathering held some interest for me, but we were so close to the waterfront I was compelled to leave the group and go wandering alone. This beach was past Sol Duc Hot Springs, rimmed by old growth forests, which echoed with far-off raven calls. The sun was warm, and La Push Beach was long and perfect for a walk right on the edge between the sand and waves. I was hopping and skipping, almost playing a game with the small surf.

Teasingly in my mind I said to the waves, *"You can't get me!"*

Suddenly a bigger wave reared up, catching me off guard, heartily splashing my legs and clothes. I ran away squealing, and when I looked down, right in the middle of a flat dry rock, as if painted by a wet finger, was the word "HA!" I burst out laughing, and was left wondering how in the world that had happened.

Wet to my waist, I strolled back to the group, sitting respectfully in the circle of people. They sat quietly on wooden chairs and large mixed-patterned pillows, listening to a humorous story about a whale told by the medicine man. People occasionally laughed, only briefly breaking their silence.

While listening to his stories, I *think* I did learn a little something: that we are not as separate from the Earth as some people may think. Our bones, blood, bodies, and molecules are formed and sustained by this planet and lit by a divine spark. He cautioned that the Earth can be fierce, or gentle, and never means to hurt us, so to be respectfully observant and careful with your fellow man and the creatures we share our lives with.

I BECAME VERY THANKFUL for learning native lessons and being open to some part of the spirit world, or angels, when one cloudy summer weekend, a good friend, her son and I headed to the Northwest Coast of Oregon. The morning was a bit rainy, but we still set up camp on grassy bluffs near the beach, next to a shallow creek gently flowing to the ocean.

After camp was set up, we took a break, and walked along the expansive sandy gray beach, speckled with shiny rocks and broken shells. Unexpectedly, we noticed thirty or more seals frolicking, barking, and rolling in and out of the waves in front of us. For some reason, my friend and I were determined to enter the water and swim with the seals. Excited and scared, we waded out into the pale green water, getting closer and closer to the hoard as they played, swam, and floated near us. We became transfixed; laughing and swimming with the seals, losing all track of time and space, while ignoring our surroundings.

All of a sudden I heard a crystal clear, very calm, but definite woman's voice say, "It is no longer safe for you to be in the water."

We thought we had left her small son safely on the beach while we swam with the seals, not noticing the current was taking us quickly away from him. I snapped out of the hypnotic fun and saw my friend's five-year-old son Casper crying, running along the beach, arms reaching out to us.

Immediately turning to Emma, I said, "We *have* to get out of the water *now!*"

As we tried returning to shore, we hit two underwater "ditches" of strong current that pulled at our legs, threatening to suck us under the surface. We trudged through the water and slippery-as-silk sand, fighting our way back to shore.

Finally, safe on the beach, we hugged her son and apologized as we watched the seals swim far away.

I was astounded, and left feeling loved, grateful, and a bit foolish since a disembodied voice had to save us that day. But I hope in the future I may be watched and warned again if I get myself into a pickle.

ONCE AGAIN, I had been protected and saved without even knowing that I was in danger. A couple of years later, I was house-sitting a small cabin set way back in woods while the owners were in South Africa. For several days, I saw a weird-looking man who gave me the willies, standing around the old, sagging, rain-soaked, mossy garage where I parked my car. He was scruffy, wore dirty clothes, and refused to make eye contact, but I felt fairly safe once I was tucked away in the cabin, reading next to the fireplace. There was no phone, no running water, and several large windows looking out into the shadowy woods. The surroundings were a bit spooky, so I kept myself busy and listened to music, trying not to worry about the strange man. I sang and danced around the living room, read, or cooked delicious meals to occupy myself during those lonely hours.

One evening, a large, fluffy, white, malamute dog showed up on the front porch whining. I had never seen this dog before. Determined not to leave, he kept begging and scratching at the door. Once it was dark and cold, I could not leave him outside, so I let him come in and decided to search for his owner in the morning. That night I could hear someone walking in the woods around the cabin cracking branches, and stopping near windows to peer inside. Thankfully the dog growled and barked several times during the night, protecting me. I hardly slept at all, huddled under my covers with a knife, intently listening to every sound. The long night slowly turned into dawn as the crickets became quieter and the birds began to sing. I groggily descended the handmade wooden ladder from the sleeping loft, then started hugging and thanking this "angel dog" profusely.

After breakfast, we walked for a good mile or so, when a frantic woman ran up to us.

"I have been searching *everywhere* for my dog, where did you find him? He *never* runs off!"

I told her of my frightful experience and how he refused to leave, guarding us through the night. Her stunned face turned into a smile as I thanked her for the protection of her sweet fluffy dog.

*Some of the best "hiding" trees grow on the Northwest
Coast of Washington State.*

Gypsy / jip-see / **Soul** / sole

A person who possesses a gypsy soul
is someone who always needs a change of scenery,
and or adventure.

Mokuna 8: **I Left My Little Island**

A fierce independence bug was biting; prompted even further by silent gray days and endless fog encased drizzle, falling through narrow windows in the dense tree canopy. A wedge started to form between myself and the love I felt for Bainbridge Island.

After many years of sadness regarding my parents' divorce and leaving Hawaii, that feeling was eclipsed by tide flats, best friends, horses, and playing in the rain. I realized going back and forth between Hawaii and Washington had given me the best of both worlds.

I had grown close to the area and bonded with many of my fellow students and teaching staff while earning a degree at the Northwest College of Art & Design; a former Irish cattle baroness's estate filled with her fabulous art collections and a beautiful burl-wood grand piano given to her as a gift.

But now I had to leave, move on, satisfy my wanderlust, and follow a misplaced crush. I moved to Colorado and to the home of my great-grandfather, who had once been the mayor of Marble. I lived in a completely different way: high in the mountains, near hot springs, hiking up sage-covered table mesas, and around dramatic red rocks jutting skyward while hummingbirds buzzed past my head. On some afternoons, thunderstorms streaked with orange lightning passed slowly along the grasslands below. I enjoyed all of the long hikes around Boulder and Chautauqua Park.

In the park, there is a particular fragrance that is like nowhere else I have been, which I can't quite place or adequately describe. It seeps up from cracks and crags in the mountains, mixing with the soil, wild grasses, and flowers. All of this is backdropped by a small burbling creek, winding cool and shaded under the trees.

Having never lived off of an island before, in my mid-twenties and feeling like an alien in this foreign land, I settled in nervously for my first snowy winter. I paid cash for a Subaru wagon, received a few quick lessons from the car dealer, and learned to drive a stick shift in one day. It came with no bells and whistles, had a slightly scratched white paint job, and the oh-so-popular *musty old car smell*—the favorite odor of all used car owners. It was perfect! Once the snow hit, I was thankful for the all-wheel drive.

I THOUGHT THAT the easiest way to move to a place I did not know was to become a live-in nanny. Having babysat quite a bit and being able to act silly enough to endear myself to children, I was hired right away. I took care of two little girls and brought them to mountain parks, walks around lakes, and ice cream parlors.

Their parents were nice at first, but that slowly changed. One breakfast morning, the mom asked what she should do with a box of stale cereal and, laughing, the dad said, "Feed it to the help," while looking straight at me. I set my sights elsewhere.

I left them a month later, after finding my own small apartment and starting work for a woman's boutique, on the pleasant open-air cobble-stoned shopping center.

If I had had to play any more children's games or clean up one more mountain of toys, my brain would have exploded anyway. So, on I went. At least working for them was a gateway to my independence.

While acclimating to living in Colorado, some thought the higher altitude was the reason for my terrible insomnia. As the night approached, my energy increased and my heart raced. It was not uncommon for me to paint large paintings while listening to music, dance around, and jog through neighborhoods in the wee hours of the night. If I ever felt nervous running alone on dark streets, I pictured rows of Hawaiian warriors running on both sides of me and was renewed with a sense of freedom and strength.

"Maybe the energy vortexes keep you awake," others said.

Having lived at sea level most of my life, I am sure I had trouble adjusting. Taking many over-the-counter sleeping pills, that I am sure were not good for me, seemed to be the only option because getting to sleep at six in the morning and having to be to work at nine just wasn't cutting it.

I was ecstatic when my little friend Kelsey tried to move to Boulder to be near me. Ironically, the first night she was there, I fell asleep at ten-thirty on the dot.

"You were just homesick," she said.

FREE RENT TO SHARE a condo with a mentally disabled woman sounded like a good idea to her. The agency said the woman, her new roommate, was child-like, simple, and nice.

Such was the case, until one dark and stormy night, when I received a panicked, hushed call from Kelsey.

"She is *crazy!*"

Kelsey was trapped in her bedroom with the woman screaming outside her door one minute and speaking softly the next, begging her in a "creepy baby voice" to let her come in. Kelsey could hear the woman having arguments with herself; changing from a harsh man's voice to her own, then to the baby's, as they fought with each other. "They" were trying to figure out how to reach Kelsey: begging, threatening, and scaring her half out of her wits.

"I am a nice little girl; I will not hurt you." then raging, "Open the door right now *bad girl!*"

I sped over, rescued her, and she quit the next day. After this incident, she decided not to stay and flew off to California to live near her dad.

I PAINTED MANY murals while living in Boulder. The first was an entire basement playroom, covered with surreal African landscapes, jungles with windows peering out into space, and an alligator crawling up the stairs, while crazy birds flew up above it. I also painted many "wall windows" (false windows looking out onto expansive views). A mural of Bison roaming on a prairie was painted for a medical supply company, and last, but not least, a mural was commissioned by a hotel in Makaha for their entryway ceiling. It was a sky view of coconut trees and seabirds which was one of those paint-all-night-listening-to-music murals that I loved.

My apartment (and impromptu art studio) was about to be turned into a Mother-in-law suite, so I moved in with a gorgeous East Indian woman near Denver. She had a coconut alter in one corner of the kitchen, and a mother who lectured her about karma every time she got a cold.

She admitted that, after being constantly hit on at bars, she started responding to the would-be-suitors in a high and screechy voice.

"My name is Sheeeenaa and I am from Innnndia Hehehehehe! That kept most of them away."

Unfortunately, it hadn't worked on a huge steroid-pumped, gun toting stripper she was dating. He "entertained" other women in the apartment every time she was out of town on business.

Did he think I would not tell her?

After I called the police to help extricate myself from one of their knockdown, drag-out fights about his indiscretions, he was escorted away while giving me a "death stare." He never returned.

Now I was working for another women's clothing store. It was exciting to be flown to Chicago and Dallas to open new stores. My tasks were to coordinate with construction workers while they finished the new store, fully stock and decorate the displays, as well as manage the staff until the newly hired manager started. When they offered the new store in La Jolla California to me, I quickly found a room to rent and started making moving plans. The mountains had been an interesting learning experience, and I had found many things I loved about the area. But, I was just dying to get back to the sea air, seagulls, fresh fish, semi-tropical foliage, and swimming in the wild blue yonder. I moved to San Diego sight unseen.

I packed quickly, assisted by my friend Liza, a woman of Northern European descent who reminded me of a prior Olympian who was no longer on their exercise regimen. Tall, strong, but soft around the edges; she was fun, creative, and fantastically funny. We stuffed the U-Haul truck full of boxes and loaded my brand-new, neon yellow Kia Rio on the trailer.

Occasionally, people relished complimenting and insulting its color: "Hey, did someone pee on your car?" or "I love that color!"

I didn't mind; my Kia was never a boring car to own and I could always find it in parking lots.

We raced out of the mountains in a flurry of snow and headed for a stopover in Vegas. The moving truck had only one direction: forward. Backing up was not a talent of either of ours or an option since we were towing my contribution to the neon culture. We stayed just long enough to see the cutest wax statues of famous actors and actresses that were much smaller than they appeared on the big screen. Some macho male heroes, if the proportions were correct, were barely tall enough to push me over, let alone fight off angry hordes while be-smeared with blue face paint. No offense. We stuffed ourselves on a huge Parisian buffet, jumped back in the truck, and headed west. The coast of San Diego or bust, or at least we *hoped* the truck wouldn't bust—no such luck.

After two days, we rolled down an alarmingly crowded California highway at night, weary, wall-eyed, and grumpy. Somehow, something went wrong with the moving truck's lights. We were driving at the breakneck speed of sixty-five miles an hour and being honked at the whole way. Liza was frantically pulling and turning the knob that controlled the lights, since they were turning themselves on and off as if possessed, until the knob broke off in her hand. We barreled down the highway in the dark with no lights. She expertly pinched and pulled at the small metal nub barely sticking out from the dashboard. Thankfully, the lights turned back on again. No more screaming women in a moving truck cab *that* night.

It took months for me to get used to the crowded highways after my smaller country roads in Colorado. They seemed more akin to frantic high-paced video games than to drivable streets. I would leave a nice following distance between me and the vehicle ahead, only to have someone "parallel" park at eighty miles an hour directly in front of me. I can't tell you how many exits I missed. This was a beautiful hill town connected by fast freeways and skirted by the ocean.

One of the first places I went was Coronado Island. I was overjoyed the first time my feet touched the ocean, sinking and wiggling my toes into the cool water and soft wave-washed sand. I was eating an incredibly fresh apple fritter just purchased from what became a much loved and visited bakery on the island.

My next favorite stop was Old Town San Diego. Just a few miles from the ocean, it was permeated with smells of fine Mexican food under statuesque and fragrant eucalyptus trees. Alluring artisan's shops selling wind chimes, pottery, and tin sculptures were around every corner. Cactuses and brightly colored tropical flowers lined the brick and wooden walkways that led to one store I always had to stop into; a quaint apothecary shop. After a quick step inside, I was delighted by all the handmade soaps and lotions. Enjoying the day with flip-flops and a breezy cotton dress on, I was truly back in my element.

On some of my much-anticipated outings, I loved to scoot out for the three hours, between the chock-o-block traffic, to and from my rental and go to a bay in La Jolla. I wore my bright orange bathing suit, snorkel and mask stuck to my face, and floated along with the flowing mermaid seaweed. Curious orange Garibaldi fish swam up to me inquiringly as if I was the mothership. After a morning of communing with the fishes, I enjoyed lying on my garish tangerine beach towel (perhaps there is a theme here) warming and drying myself on the sand while listening to seagulls, and the constant rhythm of the surf.

Once the sun was too hot, and I grew too hungry, I haphazardly threw on my sundress and walked my rumbling belly up the hill to a small café that served salads garnished with little orange cheesy fish crackers. It seemed a fitting end to my outings.

I RENTED A ROOM from a Filipino family, connecting with them and their large extended group quickly, since they reminded me of the Polynesian culture I had grown up with. Huge birthday and Christmas parties echoed with laughter and karaoke singing. It seemed as if every woman was a top-notch chef, and I enjoyed trying *most* of the traditional Filipino fare. Everything except balut, a baby chick dead and prepared in its shell. *That was just wrong.*

I bonded with many of these lovely people instantly.

One very nice and small-statured Filipino man, old enough to be my uncle, wanted to date and then marry me.

"I love big women," he would say, as he lovingly looked up into my mixed-European face, sprinkled lightly with cinnamon colored freckles that towered over him.

He tried to woo me further, allowing me to drive his white Porsche convertible to the horse races while wining and dining me. But alas, it was not a love match.

MOST OF MY experiences in San Diego were great, but some were questionable, I have to admit. For example: don't go meet a doctor in Tijuana regarding a tummy tuck, no matter how cheap it is! Unless you want a peeping Tom looking through a two-way mirror at you during your consultation. Just sayin'—not one of my finest decisions.

A friend of a friend grew up in Mexico, so one day we all played hooky from work and fled to a seaside party town south of Tijuana. Old flyers blew through the dusty streets, and the town reeked of all-night college parties. We rented some skinny horses and rode on uneven terra cotta dirt trails to the beach. Cars and partiers had caused the sand to take on a dirty, grayish appearance, and I felt sorry for the hot, bored, less-than-plump horses we were riding.

After the ride was over and my dirty white and gray speckled bag of bones was re-tied to an old fence, we ate lunch at a local hole in the wall. I was startled to notice that there was no running water in the bathrooms. Already, intoxicated men with huge drinks in their hands were stumbling around the streets.

My friends had run next door to a gift shop, leaving me to pay for lunch; of course, I had forgotten my wallet in the car.

As I went to leave, I was stopped by a panicked man blowing a whistle and yelling, "Stop lady, *pay!*"

The town must be ripe with people who "dine and dash," I thought. After a brief explanation, he let me retrieve my purse.

SWITCHING JOBS WAS EASY once I settled in San Diego. I was offered a position at a big insurance company, recommended by my landlord. A raise and a different job seemed like a good path to take. The training was intense and detailed, but I am a night owl, so I appreciated being able to work late into the night and have weekdays off. My new schedule allowed me to navigate more freely around traffic while giving more time for exploring. My wanderings took me to beaches, parks, and mini road trips up into the rolling hills. One of my best finds was a small mountain wrapped inside a river gorge near an Olympic Training Camp, that I nicknamed "my mountain."

My brother loved to tease me about that, asking, "If anyone else came to hike there too, would you run them off, yelling like a crazy person, this is *my mountain!*"

I never did do that, but the thought made me giggle.

Around the same time, my dad called to make sure I had my passport. Far off shores and bigger mountains were waiting.

The red rocks at Chautauqua Park, Colorado.

© *C.M. Arvish*

He loves to travel,

mister personality,

sandals on his feet.

Adventure dad, in front of Anna Bannana's
(misspelling intentional).

© Stepmom

Mokuna 9: **Monkeys and a Dying Elephant**

My dad was born a goofy, funny, adventurous, travel-hungry, multi-cultural enthusiast. He is known for showing up to special occasions wearing an Aloha shirt, shorts, Teva sandals, and a fake, shiny, sheriff's badge; confidently striding into any dining room, head held high, sun-bleached quaffed hair (that refuses to turn gray regardless of age or genetics) flowing in his self-made breeze, and dare-me-to-care attitude. Many a time, I hid beneath a polite and effervescent smile, my secret pride in his joyous refusal to conform to social norms or a dress code.

When I was young, he described an event to me, which by all accounts guided much of his life. He had died at the age of thirteen from a rare skin condition that caused blood infections. He rose up out of his body and recalled how clear, vibrant, and expansive he felt, floating near the ceiling, preparing to leave this Earth. As he hovered, he saw his mother crying at his side, so he decided to return, even if the confines of his ailing body made him feel heavy, sad, and groggy.

"Move to the tropics before you turn thirty or die," was the recommendation from the family doctor, since my dad's skin doesn't produce enough oils to stay healthy in dry climates.

So, once he was old enough, he sold his VW beetle, bought a one-way ticket to Honolulu, and never left. Except that is, to hitch-hike around South America with a good friend for six months, and travel around the world any chance he had.

Trying the traditional route, dad attended college for a while on Oahu. What he learned while at school was, "If you throw a party with booze and women, men will pay to attend." He left college early—had a few more adventures—and at the ripe old age of 26, opened a bar and dance club which he owned for over 30 years, in the University District. It was called Anna Bannana's, (misspelling intentional) and was named after a little girl who was said to really *be* bananas.

If a woman wanted a free bar shirt, all she had to do was pull off the one she was wearing to chants of, "t-*shirt*, t-*shirt!*" then she was thrown the design of her choice over the chanter's heads while everyone cheered.

And it wasn't uncommon for huge, bearded biker men, resembling gnarly Vikings, to read children's stories to us at the bar, while our dirty bare feet swung enthusiastically off the oversized bar stools.

Some of the perks of being the owner's daughters were free drinks (non-alcoholic) and a plethora of quarters painted red for the jukebox glowing enticingly near the front door. To this day, if I hear any of the "bar" songs like "Witchy Woman" by the Eagles, a flood of memories come back to me. I can almost taste the handmade Mexican food, Super Turkey Sandwich, a peanut butter and pineapple pizza, or the fresh hot potato skins, gooey with cheese and bacon bits, a generous dollop of sour cream on the side, sprinkled with fresh chopped chives. I ate my fine fare on one of the resin-topped tables stuffed full of postcards and knick-knacks entombed inside. Over the years, the ceiling has become festooned with license plates, posters, tennis rackets, driftwood, a deer head, neon signs, and a Budweiser lamp with the horses moving in a circle, along with and a myriad of wacky items brought in by friends and customers. The decor was topped off by an enormous hand-carved outrigger canoe strapped upside-down over the bar. My dad has never been afraid of eclectic, elaborate, unconventional décor.

Colored light and patterns from the vines growing on the exterior brick walls and an old rickshaw from some Asian country filtered through my mom's stained glass windows, occasionally sending rainbows across the floors and walls when the sun hit a beveled crystal necklace, worn by one of the regulars portrayed in her designs.

A rectangular, scratched, dented and loved sign, letters peeling, read: CAUTION EJECTION SEAT hung over the red booth where the skydivers always gathered to sit.

My dad's pride and joy, an enormous, busting-at-the-seams fish tank glowed and bubbled above the hard liquor behind the bar which was edged by brass and wood marine railing.

A GOOD TIME was had by all at the annual weeklong anniversary luau party, fondly known as bannanaversary.

Relaxed and happy adults stuffed themselves into kiddy pools out back, drinks in hand, getting tipsy and tanned, eagerly awaiting the roasted pig wrapped in chicken wire so tender its flesh would be falling apart otherwise.

Dad once pulled out a sharp pig's tooth and proudly gave the miniature trophy to me. Disgusted and with a forced smile, I took it politely. Then, when he was distracted, I hid the yellowish white trinket behind the watermelon artistically carved into a fruit bowl by my stepmom.

The day of the week when the prices of beer were put back to those of 1969 (the year the bar was opened) was particularly crazy. He kept the hordes fed with giant café table-sized pizzas delivered on the hour. The hot pizzas were served below an Anna's shirt signed by Cheech. My dad whooped and entertained the crowd, and threw free bar giveaways, as my sister and I honed our dart throwing skills in the back.

One of the grand highlights was the tattoo contest. One year the selection was not looking promising when a person called Spider-Man stepped up. He was not named for the pop culture, comic book hero reasons you may think, but because he had an arachnid tattooed on the tip of his penis. We youngsters weren't allowed to see the unveiling. The men crouched around him in eager anticipation; when, all of a sudden, their yells and expletives told us it did not disappoint as he pulled back the sheath of his uncircumcised penis, revealing the winning tattoo. It was hard to beat that one, if just for pain tolerance and shock value alone. I don't remember what he won, but I am sure my dad gave him something good.

FOR ONE OF THE bannanaversary days, a grand idea popped into my dad's head. He and some of his friends thought it would be fantastic to go fishing and bring back whatever they caught to add to the luau feast. His marine biologist buddy and his beat-up old boat were happy to oblige.

Our fishing trip started like so many other heroic and dramatic fishing stories did. Jumping in the boat, taking Dramamine, and setting off on a sunny day, smiles and high hopes abounding.

We pointed the bow towards the underwater coral cliffs off of Moloka'i and motored over swells that felt like enormous rocking horses while salt spray hit our onward-looking faces.

Once in good fishing territory, we were each assigned a large fishing pole, rotating every half hour, so it was just luck-of-the-draw who hooked a fish. There was a Japanese man from Utah, a short rotund Hawaiian man, a tall, friendly, Englishman with curly brunette hair, my dad, sister, and I. We all waited in anticipation, looking over the expansive swells and gathering seabirds.

The big strike hit! The line screamed from the fishing pole, so we all knew this was a big one. The men strapped the Hawaiian man into the center reeling chair, with the built-in white vest to keep him from flying off the boat, or being pulled over the edge. Just as he was secured, a gargantuan swordfish shot out of the water and leaped into the air.

My dad's friend, and the only onboard biologist, said, "Usually, a swordfish will either fight and jump, or dive deeper into the ocean and almost pass out, forcing us to drag the fish up to the boat before the sharks eat chunks off of it."

An hour passed before the enormous swordfish surfaced next to the boat. The wind was eerily calm, and the man was white as a ghost after fighting the huge fish for so long. I almost expected an explosion of activity, or for it to jump into the boat, thrash its huge sword around, and narrowly miss our vital organs.

The guys quickly looped a rope around its tail, as waves crashed up and down. The stern painfully bruised our forearms as we rushed to pull the fish into the boat. My heart sunk, as the fish's eye, the size of a small teacup saucer, looked consciously around at us as the men gaffed and tried to heft him up over the stern. Once I saw how aware he was of us, it saddened me that we were taking his life. The difference in his color was dramatic once he was lying in the boat dying, turning from brilliant, iridescent shiny blues with yellow accents, to a dull cold gray.

Once we were back in the harbor, he was crammed into the back of a small pickup truck and driven away to market. The swordfish was around eleven-years-old and weighed almost as much as my horse back home. The only small consolation was all the fresh tuna we were bringing back to the party, and that the swordfish was going to fine restaurants all around town.

Everyone celebrated our great success, and there were cheers all around when we arrived back at the bar, but I did not share in their enthusiasm and did not return with the guys the next year.

AFTER GROWING WEARY of years in the bar biz (no matter how fun parts of it were) and unsavory details like extortion threats, knife fights, and of course drunken people, my dad experimented with selling inflatable kayak products at the local swap meet. This grew into a thriving kayak business named Go Bananas and a partnership with the Hui Wa'a Kaukahi Kayak Club. Their proud saying, "So many islands, so little time" became a true love and passion.

Slowly moving himself away from the bar biz opened up more time for travel as well. One dangerous weapon he brought back from his many trips to other countries was a long, dark brown blow gun, with poison darts still nestled inside the hand smoothed wooden canister. He was honored to be given such an important gift from the tribe he visited, but we heard many times growing up, "*Never* touch the ends of the darts!" since he didn't know how much of the poison might still be on the lithe but intimidating weapons.

He has always been great with the "locals" per se, especially indigenous Polynesian and South American peoples, due to his funny personality and being sincerely interested in their culture and history. Once, in Tonga, during the 'King of Tonga' celebrations, some artists had painted incorrect symbols on a huge wall-sized handmade tapa cloth. *Yep*, you guessed it! They gave him the tapa. I still have the natural cloth lovingly folded and tucked away, hiding in a suitcase, just waiting for the right wall.

BY THIS TIME, my dad had avoided near misses with death a couple more times. He is adventurous, enthusiastic, outgoing, and *not* scared of dying. So it is with much delight that my sister and I can tease him about being afraid of heights. He can barely walk on an outside walkway of a three story building in Hawaii.

He will urgently tell my sister and me to, "Keep away from the edge!"

The walkways appear warped and curved to him, just beckoning for us to fall off.

Watching him flatten himself, half crouched against a wall is quite humorous since he will happily surf and swim in gigantic waves that would scare most sane people. This behavior is also surprising, after hearing stories of him swimming with reef sharks in Fiji, wading through sea-snake infested waters, and sleeping on 'Rat Island' as he and my stepmom 'lovingly' call it.

Setting up their tent was deceptively easy and fun on Rat Island, but as darkness descended on their camp, like so many insects, rats came out from hiding and started climbing their tent cords; scurrying all over their thin and fragile shelter. My dad thought it was extremely entertaining whacking at them from inside the tent, sending the rats flying. My stepmom did not think it was as funny, but at least—she recalled—Rat Island was better than when they camped in an area with huge geckos everywhere; or when they drank Kava Kava with a chief in Fiji, and suffered from the dreaded "Fijian quick step" for days (projectile vomiting and pooping). "Sometimes all at the same time," she said with a smirk.

She acted faint of heart at times. She is a peppery but innocent-looking Chicago woman and occasional pool hustler, who drove all around the United States in a camper van with her trusty German Shepherd companion. She played the role of a cockney waitress, tap dancing on tables. So, I knew she could hold her own.

After turning in her van keys, she spent many years of collegiate splendor at the Maunaolu College on Maui until finishing her degree in Mexico. While there, she had an infected tooth cut out of her gums with a steak-knife-looking device, hearing what sounded like crunching gristle, while she was shot up with some sort of questionable stimulant painkiller. This perfectly sanitary procedure was performed in a rural Mexican "dentist's" office, with farm animals and people in the waiting room outside. But *that* is another story. She moved back to Hawaii after college and settled in. Years later, she met and married my dad.

So, when my stepmom invited me to go shopping with her in Indonesia, I happily accepted of course. After hearing all their stories of far-off places around the world, *who wouldn't go*?

I flew out from San Diego and rendezvoused with her before we hopped a plane to Japan and landed on the world's only floating airport. Final destination: Bali.

Since their honeymoon years before, they have made trips back almost every year to help fill Peggy's Picks, my stepmom's eclectic antiques and collectibles shop on O'ahu.

We almost didn't go, due to the Bali bombing a month earlier at the Hilton, but we were brave and went anyway.

Since we had a long lay-over in Japan, we were eagerly met by her nephew. He had left Texas years earlier and never looked back. He is now happily married to a local Japanese woman and teaches English to businessmen. It was humorous to watch this fully Midwestern, almost cowboy type, speak in fluent Japanese.

I loved the mix of traditional and modern details in Japan. Taxi doors seemed to open by themselves, motion activated escalators came on in high-rises as we approached them, and smart lights in the hotel rooms turned on and off almost by modern magic. Our favorite futuristic toy was the toilet, of course, with its heated seat, deodorizer, half and full flush buttons, and even a little water sprayer. We each took turns playing with it, and were surprised we were not sung a little tune while on the pot.

Once settled, out we went to the countryside, on a rickety old wooden train painted dark green and covered with ornate carved details. We walked through a manicured forest and gardens, to a temple. Before entering, our hands were washed in "dragon water" as it poured from a carved stone spout. There was a sense of tradition and spiritual wonderment, as we, in quiet instinctual reverence, explored the grounds. We wandered among animal symbols, carvings, old architecture, artfully pruned trees, and enormous bells, which occasionally rung and echoed through the forest. The stark contrasts between high modernity and ancient traditions were fascinating.

On our way back to the city as we waited in an old transfer station, I heard a loud and sudden whooshing sound. Before I knew it, a bullet train whipped by, blowing my hair in a frantic swirl around my head. There weren't even any hand rails separating the fast train from standers-by. Luckily, there must be no clumsy people in Japan. I felt like it almost *sucked* me into its wake.

Our exciting day was punctuated by one of the most interesting dinners I have ever had. I cannot honestly say our meal was "good," but my cousin had the best time ordering exotic menu items we could not pronounce. He enjoyed watching our scrunched-up noses and repelled looks, as we tasted mouthfuls of fried chicken cartilage, raw who know-its, and what-its.

After much frivolity on his part, I excused myself to the bathroom. Once the surprise of seeing the choice between the literal hole in the ground to squat over, or the normal toilet wore off, I have to admit, I chose the hole. I had fun lifting my skirt, and letting it fly. I think the bathroom, for me, was the best part of dinner.

THE NEXT MORNING we boarded a comfortable flight, fully equipped with personal entertainment centers and a camera mounted on the bottom of the plane, showing views of the Philippines as we flew over. By the time we reached Bali, the streets were dark, warm, humid, and a bit scary. We headed to the "transportation" area, which was nothing more than one check-in counter and a man with a loud-speaker. There was an unintelligible squawk, followed by a dirty old black VW Jetta with no cabbie insignia which sped up to the curb in a plume of dust.

To my bewilderment, my stepmom happily said, "This is our cab" and started loading in our suitcases.

We drove, for a time, through dark old city streets, coming eventually to a splendid hotel complex surrounded by palm trees swaying under the stars, with individual huts and an open air dining area right off the beach. As the sun came up, we saw colorful Balinese boats with pointed sails, resting on pristine white sand, next to calm, crystal blue water. We enjoyed a very nice breakfast, with juicy local fruit, before walking down the boardwalk to peruse the local craft booths. When I bought a trinket, the booth owner whole-heartedly smacked the rest of the wares with the cash I had just given her as we walked away. We were offered, by local people, boat rides, tours, food, you name it, but we couldn't stop. *We* had a shopping mission.

We left the beach for Ubud (Ooo-Bood). This fun-to-pronounce, quaint tropical mountain town is surrounded by rice terraces, gift shops, temples, and the Monkey Forest. After a quick check-in and some jokes from the desk attendant about the local custom of multiple wives, we were driven up and around hills and valleys, and finally arrived at the warehouses. We were there to fill a container bound for Hawai'i and my stepmom's gift shop.

"The roads were far too crazy for us to drive," she explained, as we whipped through narrow streets and past couples with babies perched expertly on mopeds. "We only tried driving *once* and almost killed ourselves. That is when we met Putu (PooToo), and he has driven us around on every trip since. Over the years, he has also become a friend."

In one place we stopped for teak root chairs. The workers were four or five skinny teens, all dusty and shy, with a 'break room' consisting of a one burner camp cooker, a pan of plain rice, and a dirty flat bare mattress in the corner on the cement floor. Even though we were assured this was only a part-time job for them, I still wondered if they were okay. All I could think of was to compliment them on a great job making such beautiful furniture, hoping to make them feel good about what they were doing. One of them smiled and waved as we left. Putu drove us further, past ornate burial caskets covered in a plethora of colorful tissue paper and flowers. There were rearing horses, race cars, a dragon, and a big yellow bird, surrounded by incense smoke that swirled as we sped past them and continued down the road.

My mind was awash with choices after entering one after another of the large warehouses bursting with figurines, handmade paper and stick photo albums, masks and more masks, and intricate stretched out carvings of people, mermaids and giraffes. Fish wind chimes and bright shimmering sarongs spun and waved in the breeze. In front of scrolled and carved shop doors, fragrant incense wafted up from small woven leaf boxes adorned with local flowers.

Surrounded by so much Indonesian art and culture, we found deciding what to buy difficult. I was determined to find that *one* huge mask to hang on my wall right above the entryway. When I saw the "Protective Narashima Lion" (A half human and half lion known as the Great Protector) I bought the colorful and dramatic carving with bulging eyes right away. The salesperson wrapped the mask carefully and I cradled my new purchase in my arms on the return trip to Ubud.

Our hotel was small and lovely, and perched right next to the rice patties. That night we walked to a beautiful temple for an outdoor performance, set among fire torches and temple arches. Even without knowing the language, I could tell the main character was a monkey king, making me look forward to the monkey forest even more. I loved the music and the repeating *dee dee dee da la dee dee bong!* All I had to do when we got back to Hawaii was sing that, and my dad started laughing, knowing exactly what I was talking about.

Oh, the monkey forest. It was early morning when I approached the ornately scrolled gate, bought a big bunch of bananas from a woman sitting on a rock wall, and stepped inside. I thought the yellow-eyed, Doctor-Seuss-like, fluffy-faced, monkeys were cute, and then I saw their razor-sharp teeth. A group of large males surrounded me. Trying to be cheap, I gave one of them half a banana, but he grabbed onto my right leg, stopping me as I tried to step forward. He had a much stronger grip than I thought possible from his small furry hands, so I threw a full banana to the ground and ran away laughing. To my great relief, they did not pursue me, but I made sure to give only full bananas after that. I was much braver with the squirrel-sized babies and their adorable, slightly bulging eyes, and endearing Mohawk hairdos. They bounced on and off my shoulders and arms, searching inquisitively for food and treats. Many couldn't be bothered with the tourists and were happy to lounge on the intricate angles and monkey-sized steps of the ancient, expertly crafted temples. Relaxed monkeys were completely at home among the grandeur.

Wandering further into the forest, I descended a long, undulating, dragon-shaped stairway. I felt the large mossy serpentine scales bump along under my hand as I passed thick draping banyan trees and luscious-smelling flowering plants.

A small, skinny man started following me, asking, "You from New York U.S.A? Are you alone?" *Of course, I was alone,* but there was no way I was telling *him* that. Even the guide books had warned about this. They suggested saying you are from Australia or 'Australi' as I heard locals say. I found my way to the first pack of tourists, and said I was with them. He followed slowly behind, watching me for a while, and then to my great relief, disappeared.

I found my way up a small overgrown path, back to where the bulk of the tourists were. On the trail, I met a wet and disheveled female monkey, who looked picked on and crazy. She snarled at me, so I gave her a wide berth, and kept moving while reading a guidebook which explained how the monkeys were master pickpockets. With only lip gloss in my right back pocket, I did not worry about it. No sooner had I thought this, quick as lightning, the crazy female snuck up behind me and pulled my lip gloss out. She untwisted the cap and tried to 'eat' the applicator end as people laughed and took pictures. She looked like she was applying the rosy pink cosmetic to her lips.

Having had my fill of the local wildlife for the day, I casually shopped and walked back up the hill to our hotel.

One day monkeys, the next day mountains, or to be more precise, a volcano. We were headed for Mount Agung. Being from Hawaii, and knowing the reverence people had for our volcano Kilauea, I expected there would *at least* some fanfare here as well. The peak was pointy, tall, gray, and stood alone in a desolate outlying area. I might be wrong, but I got the impression there was almost a fear, or avoidance, of the mountain. Houses and people were scarce.

Our circuitous route took us over green hills, then down to a dry, rocky, and sparsely vegetated area. The surroundings were quiet and eerie. Dirt was tossed up by our car as we drove along, heading for an overlook restaurant for lunch. Around the next bend, we spotted a small woman, standing alone on the side of the road. She was maybe in her early twenties and was selling a bit of fruit, veggies, and trinkets. We could see a diminutive shack-like dwelling and an almost dead tree covered with gray dust, on the edge of a small inlet.

She said the food was from her little garden, but I could not see how anything edible could grow there. She started telling me she was married to this man who left her alone for days, and she had no way to get to town or go anywhere. Her longing for people, or someone to help her, was almost palpable. We had a quick rapport, and even joked with each other as if she was a long-lost sister. Our group was in a hurry, so all I could do was buy a piece of fruit and wave goodbye. To this day, I still wonder how she is and wish I would have been able to help her somehow.

We eventually arrived at the restaurant and marveled at the panoramic views of the imposing volcano, through large picture windows that filled the entire front of the building. Lunch was a delicious buffet, served in a fifties-style ballroom. A portion of my meal did not agree with me. Perhaps it was the delicious thirst-quenching fruit and ice slushy I drank. In hindsight, maybe it was not the *best* menu item order since we were not supposed to drink the water and it was filled with ice. I fought all the next day to force away the nausea, even through a pre-booked massage in a private room, overlooking beautiful scenery. I had the warm honey sugar scrub rubbed all over my body with nice Balinese music playing in the background. The massage would have been soothing and relaxing if I was not desperately trying not to vomit on the masseuse.

After the sticky yet pleasant massage, I was helped down two slippery stone steps and slowly submerged in a large bathtub built into the floor. The hot steaming water swirled with floating pink flower petals, and a cup of ginger tea sat enticingly in perfect reach of my right hand, just outside of the tub. The small rock and tile room was private but open to the fresh air and overlooked bright green rice fields and trees. The whole massage was only twenty dollars U.S., so I gave her a ten dollar tip. She looked surprised and thanked me with a big smile. For the price of coffee and a muffin in the U.S., I was glad to make her day.

Later in the evening (thank God after the massage), I succumbed to my nausea and vomited all night. As per my sister, I sound disturbingly similar to a dying elephant when I puke. So my stepmom, in her embarrassment, turned the volume way up on the TV so the neighbors did not think I was dying. I felt like I was, so all I ate the rest of the trip were some Hawaiian macadamia nut cookies we brought, boxed milk that was twenty-three hundred rupiah, and a hamburger at McDonald's on the way to the airport. I rarely ate fast food, but the fresh hot meal tasted delicious, and I was not worried about food poisoning there. My stepmom briefly looked up from her cheeseburger with pickles and fries, and smiled, saying, "When in doubt, eat at a U.S. chain restaurant."

I was worried about flying back through Japan, because they were quarantining anyone with a fever. They had large sensors taking body temperatures upon entry, due to the SARS (Severe Acute Respiratory Syndrome) scare.

We had one more hurdle to cross before we headed home to Hawaii: Jakarta, the Muslim capital of Indonesia, and home of the Bali bomber. My stepmom advised me to speak quietly as we landed, and headed to the customs station on our way to the next gate. We disguised our American accents the best that we could.

The gate was full of mostly Japanese travelers, except for us and three others that appeared to be backpacking students. We were just saying how we might be targets for abduction or ransom, when *boom*! All the lights went out in this, an international airport.

No one said a word, no one screamed, everyone was still and silent. We half expected to see men running in with guns to grab us. I couldn't believe that a huge international airport had lost power. A few minutes later, dim emergency lights flickered on slowly, as the room began to get warm and humid from the lack of air flow.

The usually calm and reserved Japanese flight crew hurriedly walked back and forth from the plane to the gate while speaking very quickly. We were told the plane was not fully fueled when the power went out, but they would fuel the plane as soon as possible, so we could depart. Several tense minutes later, we all boarded very quietly and efficiently, breathing a collective sigh of relief as the plane rose from the tarmac, heading swiftly towards Japan.

Luckily, they did not stop me in the airport for being sick, and the rest of the trip back to Hawaii was uneventful.

We laugh now at what happened that night in Jakarta. I still cannot believe how strange losing power was, and we count ourselves lucky that we did not end up on an evening newscast or in a hostage situation somewhere.

I now had a taste for international travel, so with the wheels turning and travel sites explored, I bought a round trip ticket for one, to Europe.

A jolly Balinese boat.
© *C.M. Arvish*

Hot chocolate mustache,
a fat man on a turtle,
illegal sausage.

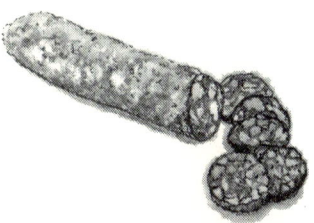

Mokuna 10: He-Who-Shall-Not-be-Named, Escorts Me to Italy

Love poems, flowers, bubble baths, massages, and romantic walks on the beach reeled me in hook, line, and sinker. I thought I had met one of the sweetest men around. It took years for the true devilish, parasitic side of his personality to seep out and smack me right in the face and consciousness. In the beginning, I was a naïve, doe-eyed puppy.

We met through some glitch in an internet dating system. My fifteen-mile dating radius somehow included Sacramento, a good five hundred miles away. Even with the distance, he-who-shall-not-be-named was set firmly on my radar. We met on December twenty-seventh; and our first picture was taken within minutes by my roommate, in front of her spinning, be-jeweled Christmas tree.

He snored like a freight train and had the toenails of a cave-dwelling troll. It seems strange looking back now, but at the time, I couldn't be bothered by those unsavory details.

Our first weekend included beach walks, Italian dinners, fudge sundaes, and a trip to the Rose Parade. He was already rhyming my middle name with his last name; which should have been another hint to run, but at the time, for some reason, I thought his behavior was cute.

A ROW OF TRAFFIC, adrenaline, and the music starting in the parade led me to jump out of my car, and lock all the doors; keys in the ignition, engine running. Embarrassed, and while we waited for AAA roadside assistance, I recounted the last time I had done this.

My friends and I were on our way to Hanauma Bay. In eager anticipation, we waited in a row of traffic before the entryway. So we would be ready to go once we parked, I went through the mental process of taking the car key off the key ring, and putting it in the watertight tube I wore around my neck. In reality, while trying to pull the key off, I hurt my thumb, and never did finish the task. Four hours later, suntanned, sandy, and still laughing from our fun with the fish, a wave of fear rolled over me as we reached the parking lot.

"*Where was the key?*" I took off running and found my dad's car still idling, keys in the ignition, and almost out of gas. Park rangers stood around ready to help; but first, they had to tease me in a nice, "Hawaiian uncle" sort of way. Once they 'broke' into the car, we coasted all the way down the hill to the first gas station. It took me years to tell my dad that I had almost killed his car. Once I did, he just got a good chuckle out of it.

I had only known 'him' a couple of months and was planning a trip to Italy on my own, so we (I) rushed his passport, bought another ticket, and that was that. If you find it a bit strange, well it was, but I was following my innocent misguided heart.

'He' was flying out from Sacramento, I from San Diego. Both of our layovers in New York were just over an hour. He did not have any extra money and was dependent on me. He came out of the airplane looking disheveled and strange. After a rushed and nervous hello, we left on our separate flights headed for the Fiumicino International Airport in Italy.

I sat next to a nice professor flying to Europe for a conference, who teased me for saying it was the first time I was "jumping the puddle."

My heart leapt as we came in site of a continent I had never seen before, and headed inland over the Alps. 'He' later described, with excitement, the Matterhorn he had seen out of his window, and the large groups of rosary-holding people on the plane, praying and clapping as they landed safely on Italian soil.

I loved stepping out into the air of another world; with new smells, sights, and people speaking in a different language. After some confusion, we found our shuttle bus to Rome. The driver dropped us off at a modest local hotel, with large shutters opening onto a stone and floral vine-covered courtyard. The tolling of church bells filled the room as I gazed out into the city. I came to love the sound of those bells.

We had the tiniest bathroom and an itty bitty shower that drained right onto the floor next to the toilet. You can't say it wasn't efficient, but maneuvering was an art of its own.

Dinner consisted of pizza from a local shop, folded, handheld, and wonderful.

We relished the cafés with delicious fresh baked crusty, but at the same time chewy, loaves of bread, a rainbow of gelato flavors, and other local foods.

In the days to come, we walked all around the city. We headed first to the Colosseum, where we were met by some rowdy Spartan warriors who wanted to take our pictures, with them of course, for a price.

We narrowly survived one sword-clad Roman warrior, who was sheathed in gold and backlit by a triumphant sun. His oiled muscles rippled, a square jaw proud and dominant, jutted out under his bristled metal helmet. With a healthy dose of Italian bravado, he strutted his manliness, while holding my disposable plastic camera.

He peered at us through the tiny square viewfinder, with his legs apart, and strappy leather sandals on his feet set firmly on the ground. With a thick, sexy, Italian accent, he said, "Say smile!"

His cohort who was brandishing a "sharp" sword and impenetrable plastic shield, yelled out, "*Kill* the Christians!"

I laughed, pointing at 'him', "*He's* a Catholic!"

Their jolly chorus rang out, "*Kill* them anyway!"

The warrior gave me back my camera and asked for 40 Euros.

Mouth agape, I shoved a twenty in his hands, and we quickly walked away. Luckily, we left them with our lives *and* pocketbooks intact.

NEXT STOP, THE ROMAN Forum, and its fantastic ruins, perfect for close up black and white photos of the elaborate carvings and architecture.

We braved the local way of crossing congested thoroughfares. "Just step out into the road, and drivers will move for you," the guidebook said.

I was scared, but, "*When in Rome . . .*" I was so happy to be able to actually say that, and be "in Rome," and it worked, we survived.

Thinking I was wiser after our warrior experience, I wasn't going to be taken again. So, of course, when a young man offered me a rose at the Trevi Fountain for free, I gladly took it, enjoying its fragrance as I walked past the magnificent statues in the water.

I soon noticed that same boy was following, and hounding my new boyfriend, "Money for the lady's rose?" Thwarted again.

Laughing off our naiveté, we continued touring the fabulous city. Rome was bursting with grandness: the Parthenon, magnificent churches, fantastic foods, mini cars, statues everywhere, two separate small beds to sleep in, and much more. The city was all I imagined it would be, and then some. I wish I had known more about the history of Italy so I could have absolutely appreciated all I saw.

At the top of the Spanish Steps, after a long fun day, we entered the Trinita dei Monti church and sat in the pews, *just* to rest for a moment. No sooner had my head touched 'his' shoulder, then a small round fiery nun read me the riot act (in Italian), telling me not to rest in the church, that "This is a holy place."

I did not need to speak Italian to understand that. I would have been quite scared of her if she wasn't the cutest little black and white nun. I hid my smile, out of respect, until we left.

THE NEXT DAY, we saw the Pontifical Swiss Guard in their flashy gold, red, and navy, striped outfits, ready to protect the Pope and what lay inside the Vatican. Every inch of Saint Michael's basilica was covered with masters' works. I could have licked the floors, it was so delicious looking. Different religious preferences aside, the Vatican was truly a marvel.

We walked past the hall of maps and their incongruous shapes, not exactly matching up with our modern topography. Next, we wound our way down narrow dimly lit staircases, and through many doors, until the room opened up into the Sistine Chapel. I was mesmerized by all the colorful figures adorning the ceiling and walls. They packed as many tourists into the space as they dared, shushing our low rumbling talking, and reminding us not to take pictures. The time went too quickly, and then we were all ushered out the other side of the room and away from the masterpiece.

Back in the basilica, I peered up at the awe-inspiring painting covering the inside of the dome. To my surprise, and after climbing many stairs to get a closer look, I was shocked to find that it wasn't painted at all, but made with innumerable numbers of shiny, bright pieces of minuscule glass, brilliantly fashioned into a detailed mosaic.

Early the next morning, away we went on a train. Next stop, Florence. We arrived in the town and emerged onto medieval streets, lined with stone buildings and ornate fixtures. We found our Bed & Breakfast easily, and were greeted by the nice couple who owned and lived in the building. The 'lift' was just large enough to fit two people, so the bags went up first. Our shower was a *bit* bigger; as long as you didn't bend over, it worked fine. Tucked in the corner of our large, lanky-ceilinged room was a small café table, framed by enormous half-opened windows. Our breakfast of pastries, orange juice, and coffee, was brought in each morning, accompanied by soft rays of sunlight and a delicate Tuscan breeze.

Slowing to the pace of this city was easy; it seemed perfectly made for outdoor market shopping, architecture gazing, and arm-in-arm meandering. We walked all day, enjoying gelato and the best thick, molten, mouth-watering, drinking chocolate I had ever tasted. Served on the side was a small plate with an opulent mound of hand-whipped cream, waiting for my spoon to swirl through it before being dipped lavishly into the dark steaming delight. Joy, for me, was a poppy seed smile, and a cocoa-cream mustache.

On our wanderings, I even rubbed the lucky bronze boar's snout that I had only seen in books. His face was worn and shiny from the countless well-wishers that visited him, but his smile remained.

The masters' sculptures, set around the city, were impressive as well.

It wasn't until we noticed the crowd laughing that we saw the street performer behind us mocking our movements, in an exaggerated way. We quickly became part of the crowd, waiting quietly and expectantly for his next victim. The woman, who found to her surprise, that she had help pushing her baby carriage by a man in garish mime clothing, was met with a chorus of crowd laughter. Next, a group of shy Japanese girls ran away, after noticing one of their friends walking hand in hand with the man like a close boyfriend. When our funny bones were amply tickled for the day, we continued onto some of the city's historic sites and churches.

At first, I was shocked entering cathedrals with elaborate gravestones in the floors. The stone effigies on the graves, which lay in the center aisleways and between pews, were worn smooth over time by people walking on them. But, when I saw an old woman kiss an ornately carved marble tomb, set in the wall topped by an immaculate statue, I understood how much respect and love she had for the departed.

What can I say about the fantastic, red, green, and white stoned Duomo, smothered with frescos and gleaming tiled scenes far above in its cupola? After climbing ancient stairs that appeared more like marshmallows than stone, and an aerobic exertion, the reward was to be nose to tile with the sumptuous mosaics. This was topped off by a breathtaking 180-degree view of the city. We peered down as people enjoyed their day, strolling in the large square, past intricate and ancient structures, holding gelatos and holding hands.

Our very first Valentine's Day as girlfriend and boyfriend was spent in the lush Boboli Gardens; found just over the golden bridge, past artists selling watercolor paintings of the sunflower-strewn Tuscan countryside. I still cannot believe I did not grab one of the gorgeous panoramic scenes as we walked by, much like at the Vatican gift shop, when I had decided not to purchase a beautiful silver cross. *As if I could just go back there, like it was a department store*, I still tease myself.

Once in the gardens, I was entranced with the long colonnades and slowly undulating stairways, edged by immaculately trimmed foliage. Fountains in the middle of ponds, which sprayed water into the air, punctuated the splendor. Perfect classical bodies carved out of stone were placed all around the gardens, but my favorite, I have to admit, was the large rotund man sitting on a larger-than-life turtle near a moss-covered cave. We spent time walking through the grounds, sitting on benches, reading love poems to each other, fingers entwined as if we were super-glued. It all seems pretty funny to me now.

A couple of days later, we reached what would become my favorite city in Italy: Venice. The gorgeous buildings, churches, and interlocking bridges, were surrounded by waterways and boat taxis. I loved to get lost, roaming past street vendors, and winding our way through narrow cobble-stoned passageways, and over small arching bridges. We didn't even mind, not knowing how to find our way back to our hotel most of the time.

We arrived in Venice just as the carnival was starting. In St. Mark's Square, people wore elaborate costumes and feathered hats. Puppet shows and music surrounded us, as groups of masked people celebrated undeterred. The scene was a kaleidoscope of smiles, spinning dresses, joy, and frivolity. One man wore high-heeled Victorian shoes, small feathered wings, and a white wig. He proudly strolled past us with a woman on his arm, who was dwarfed by the brightly shimmering, voluminous dress she wore. Once the sun set, the revelers took gondolas lit by lanterns, to dine in water-edged restaurants wafting with the fragrance of fine Italian food and fresh bread.

I bought a feathered mask to wear, and 'he' a Casanova hat, so we could, in some small way, be part of the celebration. We did not have enough rhinestones, or velvet on, to play the roles properly, but we enjoyed the atmosphere none the less.

Swept along by all the festivities, we decided to splurge by dining in a deluxe restaurant on a canal, where I ordered the "special fish dinner." A wide-rimmed white dish was proudly placed in front of me. This was quickly followed by my internal laughter and shock. What I saw on my plate looked like random crispy tiny bait fish, scooped from the canal, deep-fried, with eyeballs intact, staring up at me. My boyfriend's dinner was wonderful, so I politely pushed around the 'food' on my plate, pretending to enjoy it until we could leave. Then, I headed straight for the first pizzeria I could find, giggling (at my freaky fish dinner) as we walked down the cobblestone streets set aglow by vintage light fixtures.

Of course, we had to ride in a gondola *at least* once. So, after I had devoured the pizza, we headed for the moored gondolas, bobbing slightly in the canal. After we precariously boarded, the gondolier oarsman in his black and white striped shirt and hat, sang as he rowed us through the dark shimmering canals, past covert side entryways, and gaudy baroque terraces.

In the morning, it was one of the wooden water taxis which took us through small slapping waves to the glass-blowing island of Murano. We saw artisans making a variety of blown glass pieces, from ornate masterpieces to small tourist trinkets. *Again,* I did not buy something. *I must have had some sort of brain issue.* Before leaving Venice, finally I bought a glass gondola, and some hard Italian sausage to take home with me. It was back in the states, accompanied by a bit of irony, that I *finally* found a lovely blue vase with its golden 'MADE IN MURANO' sticker still attached. *This time*, I bought the vase.

Luckily, our farewell meal in the restaurant below our hotel was fabulous: mineral water, fresh bread, and delicious baby clam linguine. We had perfect weather for our entire trip in Italy. But, on the last day in Venice, we woke up to a powdering of snow as a departing gift.

Back in New York, waiting for my connecting flight, I leaned against a railing, tired, sore, and trying to stretch away the hours of sitting in a cramped airplane seat. All of a sudden, I was approached by a small hound dog pawing at my bag. At the end of his leash was a stern-looking airport security woman, staring at me accusingly.

"What is in your bag, Miss?" She asked, in a commanding deep southern accent.

Nervously I opened it.

They had *found* the Italian hard sausage.

"Ma'am, you can't bring this into the United States, it must be surrendered."

I handed it over and decided that they just wanted good Italian meat with their lunches, and had used their special "sausage police doggy" to find it. I wonder if he ever got to have a piece.

For some reason, I couldn't find any pictures of our trip to Rome, without 'his' face torn out.

© C.M. Arvish

Even through the thickest fog,

eventually, the sun,

and the truth,

come out.

Mokuna 11: **Quicker than a Las Vegas Wedding**

The move to Sacramento was easy. I was hired, promoted, and given a raise, all in one week. The last company I worked for, had a boot-camp-like training regime, and was known for its high employee turnover. If I could last there, then I would excel with this new company. I moved into 'his' apartment, where he was given reduced rent for being the maintenance manager, and we settled in. We lived next to a long river and enjoyed bike rides, leisurely walks, and kayaking on warm days.

He was fired from the pleasant riverside apartment complex months later after he was found sleeping on the job in empty units. With his terrible credit, I could not find an apartment to rent within fifty miles of Sacramento, so I scrambled, and bought us a townhouse.

You would have thought my loans were written by a gold-toothed, shifty-grinned, curly chest-haired, polyester shirt-wearing, loan shark. In actuality, it was by a professionally-dressed, clean-cut person from a large, well-known banking establishment. In my naiveté, I expected that great credit and a good job insured me a proper loan, but it turned out to be the opposite.

"This is what all people have to do when buying a house," he said, with a glimmer in his eye, to the $200,000 first mortgage, and the three-year $57,000 second mortgage, equipped with a balloon payment and high-interest rate.

Conveniently, whoever set up my loan checked my credit score twice, so that they could add an even higher rate to the second loan with the balloon payment.

"It's *no* problem. You have such good credit, you can re-finance in six months."

I even had the old tax switcheroo pulled on me. Sitting in the office of the title company, the woman processing the paperwork flashed me a giddy chipper smile and said, "Oh darn, they didn't use the correct year for the taxes when writing up your documents." After a few gleeful quick taps on her calculator, my house payment went up another two hundred dollars a month.

With my budget already stretched, hot tears and anger quickly welled up and poured down my face. I called my realtor.

He defensively and loudly spoke back to me, "Are you questioning my integrity?"

What I *should* have said was *yes*, but he continued.

"It is too late to back out now. You *could*, but then the seller can sue you. You wouldn't want that to happen, would you?"

I signed the seemingly endless stack of papers, and went on my way.

I put all the drama of buying my townhouse aside and tried to enjoy our new place. It was nice, but a bit dated, so I soon re-painted, glass-tiled the bathrooms, and added Venetian plaster to the main wall in our living room. Finally, it felt like home.

Never again in my life—if I can help it—will I have homeowner's association dues. A woman, resembling Cruella Deville's twin sister, drove around the complex slowly, slinking past the homes in her black town car. With mid-century glasses perched low on her nose, and a clipboard in hand, she scanned the complex, trying to find any little infraction to fine a homeowner for.

Even rules broken by the previous owner were quickly billed to us. I came to call the association board "witches from heck," but I am sure you can imagine more colorful terms.

Life in general seemed to be going fairly well, but God *knew* I was going to need an angel. With some insistence, my boyfriend told me that 'he' wanted a dog. Initially, I did not, but I have to admit to being thankful for his persistence. We found Sunny dog in an animal shelter in Grass Valley, on our way to go hiking one day. I was looking for a small dog, but this bigger one that appeared like Lassie without all the fluff, looked out of the cage at me, without so much as a sound. I had never seen a smooth-coated Collie before. We passed him by, but a feeling in the pit of my belly was urging me to go back to him.

I kept repeating, "What about him? What about him?"

My boyfriend wanted a more macho dog, but I persisted, and thank *God* I did. We pet him outside as he rubbed up against us. He was rated as "family and kid safe," but the paperwork said he was "owner-returned" because he chased cats and was too affectionate and sickly. I was nervous, but we took him anyway, straight from the cement-lined oppressive cage to an open trail with fresh air along the North Fork of the American River, near Auburn.

We bonded immediately, and became attached at the hip. While hiking, I 'asked' him what his name was (in my head) and quickly heard it: Sunny, matching his bright orange Collie coat, long funny nose, and joyful personality. I thank God, the angels, and nature spirits every day for guiding me to him. It is so sad that he had to be trapped in that cage, but somehow I listened and was able to take him home with me. I had no way of knowing, when I found him, that he was going to save me, maybe even more than I had saved him. I cherish him for his kind, sweet, protective nature.

As it turns out, he wasn't sickly or badly behaved, or any of the nonsense the previous owner had written down. She was just the wrong person for him, and I was the right one. My relationship was progressing with my boyfriend too. On our first visit to see my family in Hawaii, he asked me to marry him at sunset while we sat on Kaimana beach, and I said yes.

A YEAR LATER, after all the plans and arrangements: airplane tickets, wedding chapel, and honeymoon details, he mentioned six weeks prior to our nuptials that he was, "Not legally divorced from his previous wife yet." I was just a *little* angry, so he rushed the divorce papers, but to no avail. In California, there is a mandatory waiting period of six months before you can re-marry. So, in Hawaii, I had to sit there with my mouth closed as I heard him lie over and over again, telling everyone this was his first marriage. I was too embarrassed to tell my parents, so we had a fake wedding.

We were not back from our honeymoon on Maui for a month, when one Friday morning, five minutes before I was leaving to work, he stopped me and said, "I bought a car for my ex-wife, and I am driving it to Southern California for her."

I didn't have time to react before he was out the door; this, from the man who couldn't help me pay the mortgage, or most of our bills. He, and his ex-wife, even had the gall to call me together and ask to be put on our car insurance. Because he was the registered owner of her new car and we already had an insurance policy together, with my back against the wall, I agreed. I felt like he had cheated on me with his ex-wife. Upon his return, and with a set jaw, I listened to his excuses, and for some reason, forgave him.

Possibly for love, or because he was a *man*, I thought I was supposed to set aside the personal strength and spiritual knowledge I had gained as a child. I ignored my female intuition and held back my opinions, so I wouldn't make any waves and became a constant provider and achiever.

At the same time, I was slowly being indoctrinated into his religious group, in which I was shamed out of my female power and fortitude. He even went so far as to say that women were the ruin of man. His friends mentioned, during a religious study at our house, that some of my paintings of partially nude tropical women, and dancing crows, looked evil. I was stunned. "It couldn't be further from the truth," I said, but they were not interested.

I lost myself, and because of it, I was paying the entire mortgage, all the credit cards, taking us on trips, and not having the boundaries to say no.

If you have figured out by now that putting all the bills in my name, paying for our trips, our entertainment, and our expenses was not a very good idea, then good for you. It took me a little longer. In my defense, my close friends and family members never took advantage of each other, so I didn't have experience with this type of person before, being a very trustworthy and kind person myself. In our relationship, I gave and gave, and he took and took. It was perfect for him.

As if I had not been a big enough doormat, I even let him move his ex-stepdaughter in, so she did not have to live with her drug dealer father. Yes, I was a sucker for a sob story, always wanting to help. They said she would pay rent. That lasted *maybe* two months. The final straw was when she started allowing her nasty friends to party and get drunk in my house. After they threw cigarette butts all over the landscaping, I cracked. When I told her to move out, my pseudo-husband asked if she could take my "extra" TV and bed with her from the guest bedroom. They were *very* angry when I said no.

"You are so selfish and greedy," he scowled.

Next, I had to take back the co-signed credit card. He over-drafted the limit and hid the unpaid bills from me.

I got my own P.O. Box and forced him to give back his credit card to me. The next month, I was shocked to find many new charges on that same card.

When I asked him about it, he became angry and defensive, "*Why* are you are questioning me like I'm a bad child, don't you trust me?" Finally, he explained how he had written down the credit card number from a bill, but stopped using it after he lost the piece of paper.

At the same time, I found out that no one would re-finance my mortgage. Call after call I heard the same response.

"Your debt-to-income ratio is too high, maybe wait several years, and then try again."

Remember that balloon payment? "I won't sell you a bad investment." That statement from the real estate agent kept ringing in my ears.

They knew they were signing me up for a foreclosure, and must have seen the neon "sucker" sign on my forehead from a mile away. I couldn't even rent it and move, when I found out the same townhouse next door to me was rented for almost nine hundred dollars a month less than my mortgage. 'He' said he did not want to move anyway.

Finally regaining some strength, I said, "Neither would I, if I was living here for free!"

He did not reply.

I tried to carry on, while pulling money from my 401k to keep us afloat. I attempted to short sell the townhouse, but no one came looking. The housing market was in the middle of crashing, so everyone was waiting for rock bottom to hit.

To make matters worse, I had a $200,000 life insurance policy, and 'he' was the beneficiary. I had heard that was what married people did.

Soon after I bought the policy, we went on a camping trip, and he teased me in front of his disgusting, drugged-out, ex-stepdaughter while we were getting our inflatable kayak ready for the lake. He looked me straight in the eyes and said, "Wouldn't it be fun if you died or drowned so that I could have the insurance money?"

His ex-stepdaughter smiled her snaggletooth grin at me, and said, "*I'd* take half of that."

I was scared the whole time kayaking on the lake, imagining him thinking up ways to dispatch me—especially when he maneuvered us back into this narrow remote grotto. I thought he might try to drown me or make some sort of fatal "accident." For some reason, I was powerless to stop what was happening. I didn't know how to *not* go kayaking with him, or take off in the truck and leave him far behind, or swear at him and file for divorce. I just sat there, in front of him in the kayak, vulnerable, and passive. His holier-than-thou façade revealed a darker and darker soul hiding within, and I wasn't sure what to do.

Weeks later, when I discussed separating from him, he paused and asked, "Where would I live?"

With brow furrowed, I asked in reply, "Do you even love me?"

After a long pause, all he could come up with was, "Well, you *are* quirky."

It sank in that he never loved me. He just loved all the stuff he could get from me, and I gave a lot.

That is when the nightmares started. Demons paced around our bed at night, ripping down the decorations I had put up, and stomping on them. I moved myself into the guest bedroom, and held tightly to Sunny dog through the long dark nights.

I had told very little of this to anyone, since I hated asking people for help. But then, my sister Joanna called me in alarm, describing vivid nightmares of me telling 'him' that I was leaving, and in a fit of rage, he gripped his hands around my neck and strangled me. Then, he came to and panicked, since he had just killed me, while a demon—delighted that its plan had worked—paced back and forth at the bottom of the stairs.

I took her warning very seriously.

At the same time, he was continually making passive aggressive comments about how Sunny dog did not want to go with me that he loved *'him'* best, and he would keep him, knowing how much taking Sunny would torture me. In a very short time frame, he became disgusting-looking, with red patches growing on his midsection and back, pimples on his scalp, and an evil look in his dark gray eyes. I knew I had to get myself and Sunny away from him as quickly as possible.

I concocted a plan.

The plan was to pretend that I wanted to go camping at Lake Tahoe for the weekend. I asked him to go on ahead, set up camp, and we would arrive later with all the food and fixings.

I had pre-rented movers and a large truck. Unfortunately, the home owner's association had decided to black-top our driveways the same day I was making my retreat, so the movers had to painstakingly haul my belongings out to the main entrance. This made the already tense and scary process feel like an eternity to complete. My heart jumped every time the entrance gate to the duplexes clanked open. I dreaded seeing the turquoise truck, metal grill, and his furious gaze staring back at me. The movers slowly ferried my belongings with carts and hand-trucks along the rutted sidewalks, like a ticking, clock of doom, past several other townhomes, back and forth from the exit.

Sunny waited patiently inside for me. If I saw 'him' I would only have a couple of minutes to run inside, grab Sunny, race out the back door, sneak behind other townhomes, and jump in my car before he could reach me.

Finally, the movers finished. With an anxious heart, I loaded my most precious possession into my car, took a last wary look at the complex in my rear view mirror, turned the key in my ignition, and followed the movers far across town, to the secret apartment I had rented for Sunny and I.

I was scared the whole time moving that he'd figure out why I wasn't at the lake and race home to catch me in the act. Luckily, he did not. He came home the next day to an empty house. I saw later, when I snuck back to grab my bike, that he had trashed the place.

Soon after my retreat, dad came from Hawaii for a month to help me unpack and keep my evil pseudo-husband away. We saw 'him' slowly passing us in his truck, and watching us eat dinner at local restaurants from the parking lots. He had been driving around trying to find me. He left phone messages telling me that everyone was praying for me to return to him, since the "enemy" had taken me away, and that God hated people who get divorced. He ended his calls by saying, "The wedding rings on our fingers mean you can't leave me." The next call I answered, and told him—to his surprise—that God had helped me get away from him, and did not want me to stay with such a horrible, two-faced person. He was silent.

MY HOUSE QUICKLY went into foreclosure. But I knew, if I had not bought the house, that I would never have found Sunny dog, so it did not seem so bad. I called him my $257,000 dog, and he was worth every penny—actually, he is priceless.

I was starting to feel happy again, living with Sunny in our new vaulted ceiling apartment. It was situated on a hiking and biking trail that skirted the river near Old Town Folsom. I enjoyed eating at local cafés after wandering through gift shops, even though I always had a feeling of being watched. He called me constantly, begging for me to return. I don't know why he could manipulate me so well, but in a foolish moment of weakness, and to my family's great dismay, I agreed to small visits and occasional dates.

My angel Sunny dog.
© C.M. Arvish

Could I have stopped it?
I never saw it coming.
Someone, please help me.

Mokuna12: **It Happened**

I had no way of knowing that, in a just a few hours, my life would be changed forever. My stiff and sore neck had lasted a week. "*It must be stress*," I told myself. So, I booked a massage after work, on Friday the 21st of December. During the massage, I was lying on my back, when the massage therapist pushed my head up, chin to my chest, pushing and twisting while he did it. All of a sudden, part of my spine felt like it popped, ripped, and tore in the back of my neck.

He sat me up, to test my "range of motion." It felt like someone had sliced the length of my left arm open, and threw acid inside. My left hand fluttered, stung, and buzzed wildly.

The massage therapist dismissed my description and questions, quickly saying, "It's just your nerves waking up, go home and take a hot and cold shower."

I was so used to being worried about my pseudo-husband; I didn't anticipate an assault coming from a completely different direction.

After paying, I started the five-minute drive home. The pain got worse and worse every minute. I parked haphazardly, and barely made it up the stairs.

I climbed into the shower, as I was instructed to do. "Take a hot and cold shower," the massage therapist had said. I tried to stand in the hot water but crumpled uncontrollably onto to my knees.

Facing the back wall, I tried bracing myself on trembling arms, the increasing horror and pain of what was happening to me piercing my mind. After crawling out of the shower, I could not towel myself off, and ended up belly down on the bathroom floor, naked. With eyes closed, I lay on the floor, hardly able to move, and in so much pain I did not know how I was going to survive. I begged for 'him' to call an ambulance, but he *refused*!

He had appeared a few minutes before, with take-out dinner, and found me suffering in the bathroom. With his heavy, unsympathetic palm on my upper back, he prayed over me. When I wasn't instantly better, he accused me of not having a "good enough faith in God."

He did not want me to call the paramedics since it was going to embarrass him to have them see me undressed. Barely able to move, with excruciating pain engulfing me, I mustered all the strength I could and yelled at him to give me the phone. He relented. With eyes pinched tight and my face on the floor, I spoke the best I could to the emergency service.

After just a few minutes, two nice paramedics arrived. Gingerly, they slid stretchy pants up my legs, and draped my soft, pink, Hawaiian lavalava wrap over my shoulders. I could not use my left arm, and had to cradle it to my chest like a baby. The paramedics used their gurney chair to carry me down the stairs, and we were off, sirens blaring. In a haze of pain, we arrived at the ER. Tears streaked down my cheeks. The IV medications did nothing to calm the torment going on inside me. Surrounded by nonchalant onlookers, I was unable to articulate my suffering.

As they sat me up for x-rays, uncontrollable sobs took over, shaking me as the weight of my shoulders crunched and compressed my already tortured nerves. I had to stay as still as possible, forcing back any movement, as they repeated and repeated the x-rays since most were blurry from my sobbing.

"Go see your family doctor for an appointment," was the final recommendation.

Doctors sent me home with a prescription for oral medications at midnight. My pseudo-husband complained the entire drive about how long 'he' had to sit in the ER, and that *he* was tired. So, annoyed, he dropped me off at my apartment and left me alone.

I was in more pain than you would wish for your worst enemy to feel for a minute, let alone an hour, but it continued, around the clock, 24 hours a day, relentless and with no mercy.

For the next few days, I lay on my beige living room floor, barely moving, trapped inside a horrible cocoon of misery, not knowing how I could feel that much pain and survive. My left arm stayed held to my chest. Pillows hurt, my bed hurt, and moving was intolerable. Sunny dog periodically lay down gently next to me, sniffed my face, or licked my tear-streaked checks. I am not sure how, or if I fed him. My eyes were clamped shut most of the time. Only a few things changed as the days passed, and I held myself as still as possible. It was either light or dark outside of my sliding glass door, next to the unlit Christmas tree.

I could barely eat, since it caused more pressure as my stomach filled, and increased the intensity on my crushed nerves. I swallowed handfuls of dangerous oral medications that barely touched the pain. It was terrifying each time my so-called husband came to walk Sunny dog. I was so afraid he might steal him, but I had no control. I thank *God* he did not.

I couldn't even cry, as every twitch, and every move, caused a searing intense pain.

AFTER HEARING OF MY plight, my sister Joanna urgently raced to California from Seattle. Her eyes were fixed to the road, burdened by an ominous feeling that I was on the border between life and death, and she wanted to make *sure* I stayed.

Early the next morning, after struggling to my ringing telephone, I heard my mom's concerned voice. "Your sister is around the corner from your apartment, she will *be there* soon, just hold on."

At that point in our lives, I barely knew my sister or talked to her. Growing up, our personalities were like oil and water, but she had dropped everything to come to my aid. After her arrival, on December 26th, she found the only medical facility open around Christmas: an acupuncturist. Desperate for whatever might help, we went to this kind, little, old, Armenian man's office.

It was with immeasurable patience that she was able to help me, ever so slowly, down the steps and into the car. Every step was unbearable, and jarred my nerves. I had to ride in the car lying back in the seat, as she took corners, accelerated, and braked as gently as possible.

In a minor miracle, the acupuncture relieved *some* of the torture across my left shoulder blade, allowing me to sit up a bit better. All the pain and horror was still there, but even a little relief was something.

She had to bathe me, dress me, and feed me, because I was mostly bed-bound. She cut my hair off, so she could wash and brush it easier.

I desperately wanted some comfort, some relief. I couldn't fight, I couldn't scream, I couldn't run. I was completely powerless, and just had to lie there and accept what was happening to me. Even showers were excruciating since hot water burned the hypersensitive nerves in my arm, as they continued their rapid alarms.

Later, a chiropractor said to me, "Your nerve root space was obliterated."

It was as if someone had cut through my neck, and was standing on my smashed nerve without stopping. I wondered if I was going to be able to ride a horse, kayak, rappel into a cave, swim, dive, or paint huge murals again. Realizing that much of my identity and pride in myself came from being physically strong and adventurous, it was a hard and scary pill to swallow, that just simple tasks had become difficult or impossible for me to do.

The oral medications were so harsh they caused me to vomit blood. I don't know if you can imagine what it was like, to barely be able to move, then have to go as quickly as possible from your bed to the bathroom, while your body violently convulses as you throw up. I strained with every muscle, trying to stifle the painful, involuntary movements, thinking I might die, as I collapsed next to the toilet.

Some days the torment was so much, that all I could do was stare at my sister, tears streaming, choking back sobs, as the minute shudders of crying sent me over the edge with suffering. She would gingerly help me into the car and race to the urgent care.

As I sat on the doctor's table, still and quiet, forcing back any small exertion, I must have been hard to read. Joanna had to demand that the urgent care doctor listen to her. She said assertively, "We *do not* show pain like other people, *please* help my sister!"

I was so thankful how she fought for me, since I could barely speak for myself, or articulate my suffering, as my brain shut down, my words periodically slurred, and I lost my focus with the constant near-death intensity of pain. Next, my memory became shot. My mom and I later decided that there was no way my mind could retain the memories of the prolonged agony, as a defense mechanism, or I might have cracked.

I am still "wonky" to this day, but as Kelsey loves to remind me to lighten the moment, "Ah, you were weird before this happened."

One shot in the right butt cheek for pain, one in the left for nausea, and we headed home. I cannot describe the utter internal joy when the pain subsided a little, and I could get more than a few hours of sleep. Joanna had to continuously care for me, while we waited the mandatory month until my medical insurance would pay for an MRI, since the ER had taken x-rays.

I HAD NEVER KNOWN who my sister was before this, or realized how caring, and maternal she was, and how devoted she could be. I rarely connected to my brother Tatum either, who was many years younger than I was. With me having the will of a horse, and him, the crazy energy of a monkey boy, we didn't always see eye-to-eye. He was not happy unless he was snowboarding 100 mph down a mountain with his ginger hair on fire, and described himself as naturally caffeinated. With kindness, he still called to see if he could help in any way, and if I needed, he would try to keep my pseudo-husband away. Having left home so many years ago, I hardly kept in contact, being a fiercely independent woman who never wanted help from anyone. I didn't realize how that had caused me to distance myself from most of my friends and family. It was so touching that they still cared for me, after I had basically abandoned them. In a heartbeat, I was turned from an independent adult, to a dependent child, with nothing to do but accept the love and care they were giving me.

AFTER CHRISTMAS, MY DOCTOR prescribed physical therapy. Well, that didn't work out too well. They could barely touch me, and one woman became angry with me, saying, *"Stop* holding your arm, you are just *perpetuating* your injury."

If I straightened my arm, the sensation was akin to pulling a rubber band, laced with nerves, almost to a breaking point. At the same time, it strained and screeched with pain. When my movements caused terrible pain, I was told on my next visit that they couldn't do anything for me, and to go back to my family doctor. After I went back to my doctor, the staff appeared frustrated and got snippy with me when I described how horrible physical therapy had been.

This sharp-faced physician's assistant quoted the notes on all three days, and said each note simply read, "Patient tolerated treatment."

If they only knew how much *I did not tolerate it at all.* But, they wouldn't listen, so, I was sent home with more pain meds, and no resolution. We were still waiting to do the MRI.

It was hard to understand why they were so angry with me. It was like being upset at someone who had lost their fingers, since they couldn't grow them back. Because my injuries were hidden on the inside, they couldn't actually see the amputation of my life as I knew it, and the loss of physical abilities we all take for granted that I loved and counted on.

Again, my sister, and family who lived far away from me, were left to find treatments that could possibly help, since my doctor and his staff did not seem interested in helping.

In a coincidence, my sister noticed a chiropractic office with a sign in the window that read, "Spinal Specialist." On my first appointment, this kindly chiropractor took the time to listen and gently examine my neck, seeming to understand the severity and complexity of what had happened to me. He was appalled that I was still waiting for an MRI, and ordered it right away. When we met later, he showed me the devastating films.

He looked at me sympathetically as he said, "I am very sorry that this has happened to you, but I do not have the equipment or expertise to help properly."

A wave of shock came over me as we viewed the large gray blob on the MRI film, pressing on my nerve root, showing the severe disc rupture.

While working in the auto insurance industry, I spoke to many clients with spinal fuses due to disc ruptures—we called them "egg shell people." They were prone to having more ruptures around past spinal fusion locations, in minor to moderate motor vehicle accidents, and in rare cases the fuse had caused paralysis. So, of course, I was terrified of undergoing that very dangerous surgery. As the days turned into weeks, my sister and mom continued looking for a less invasive procedure.

Laser surgery was $30,000 out-of-pocket, so that wouldn't work, and insurance wasn't covering disc replacements in the U.S. yet. Paying for, and flying to Europe for, the procedure was out of the question. It seemed to me, fusions were being handed out like lollipops, but less invasive surgeries were harder to find. Our search continued.

IT TURNED OUT my mom's world-class naturopath, from Medford, Oregon, had successfully treated disc ruptures with Colchicine. Used as far back as Roman times, it is a powerful natural anti-inflammatory, and had kept many of his patients from needing spinal surgery. The biggest hurdle would be getting me there. After a trip to the urgent care for pain injections, we would have a narrow four-hour window to fly me to Oregon. Someone would have to be ready to grab me from the airport in Medford, and rush me to another urgent care, or straight to bed.

The race was on.

Two shots in the butt, and my sister hit the highway.

I made it through the first flight, landing safely in San Francisco. While waiting at the next gate, I noticed something was wrong. As the time approached for our flight to board, we had not been called yet.

The flight had been delayed.

I sat there holding my left arm, trying to breathe through the pain, waiting anxiously to board the next flight. Desperately hoping we would be allowed to embark soon. With every minute, my pain medication continued to wear off, and my suffering increased.

Then the announcement came over the loud speaker, "Your flight has been canceled."

I was stuck in the San Francisco airport, pain ramping up and up, every minute, with nowhere for me to go. After calling Joanna, she and her visiting husband started driving immediately, but they were at least three to four hours away in traffic. I desperately needed to lie down, but there was nothing. By a stroke of luck, her husband was in the military. He called the USO, a special room for military travelers only, and they said they would let me in.

The room was a long walk away. It was becoming harder and harder for me to think or focus, so I attempted to stop a motor cart to take me.

I tried explaining what was happening, but the driver, barely looking my way, kept on going, and said, "You're almost there."

Almost there, for me, was akin to miles away in that moment. Every step pounded on my nerves as I walked. I did not have the strength to try to find another cart. Tears flowed, unrestrained, down my face, as I stepped forward moaning in agony. I couldn't even care, or think what people may have thought of me, and no one seemed to notice.

I finally arrived, and the only position I could find any bit of comfort in, was lying upside down on a lawn chair styled piece of furniture with my legs crossed, knees sticking up in the air. The last image I remember was a woman looking at me, with a disgusted look on her face, before I lost consciousness.

Hours passed before I was awoken gently by my sister touching my shoulder. I was so thankful for that military room. They helped me to the car, and we started the long drive home, and to bed.

Oregon was no longer an option, so my sister diligently searched and found a chiropractor with a spinal decompression machine. Their office was only half an hour away from us in a quaint little town called Auburn, and they could see me immediately.

"The longer the nerve is compressed, the more likely you are to have permanent damage," the doctor said.

Since my medical insurance did not pay for this "experimental" procedure, my mom paid for the first $5,000 on her credit card, and they started helping me.

With my head firmly fixed into a cradle, strap squeezing my forehead, and nondescript music softly playing, the decompression machine slowly started trying to suck part of the disc rupture back in. It pulled and released over and over again, using a computer-guided program. Many visits ended in tears from the strain of just showing up and going through the treatment. But, slowly, over many weeks, I started to make some progress. Being able to sleep a bit more, and ease myself a little better on and off of the treatment table, was a small but welcome improvement. Simple tasks were still a struggle most of the time, but, ever so slowly, some range of motion started coming back.

They were kind and gentle with me there. They even attempted to improve my left hand and arm which had an odd sensation, as if it was wrapped in duct tape, and the lightest touch resembled painful sandpaper scraping against my skin.

MY SISTER HAD taken care of me for several months, but eventually she had to go home. Without her help, I was forced to carefully drive to the grocery store for a few small items, or up the long winding road for decompression treatment. Changing lanes or backing up was precarious, because of my limited range of motion. Sunny dog had to settle for very short walks around the apartment complex.

I wish Joanna could have stayed longer for many reasons, but especially because she had kept he-who-shall-not-be-named away. This was particularly evident one day when 'he' came over to walk Sunny, and wash my hair. Now that I had no one else to assist me, he said that he would come over some days and help me with showering, cooking, and other daily tasks.

As soon as I stood under the showerhead, I saw his real intentions, set as firmly in his mind, as in his newly swollen male member. To him, I was no more important than a blow-up doll covered with flesh.

He chose, wrongfully, to twist his religious and personal beliefs, and reminded me of my duty as a wife to have sex with him, and that displeasing your husband is displeasing to God. I was nothing more than property or an indentured servant to him, only there to serve his needs, regardless of my displeasure, or suffering.

So, after years of emotional blackmail, brainwashing, and silent shackles tightening around my wrists and ankles; in situations such as these, it left me unable to protect myself, or have the voice to say no. Trying to be amorous and somewhat romantic, he sucked on my right earlobe, but his heavy breathing, and slightly stuffy nose, repulsed me.

Sex with him was not a consensual act, but an act of fear. I was afraid if I did not comply, he would not help me, afraid of repercussions or punishment, afraid of displeasing him, or afraid he would hurt Sunny. I just wanted him to stop and go away, so I could climb into bed with my unwashed wet hair, Sunny dog by my side, and slip into a painful oblivion.

BY THIS TIME, my corporate short-term disability coverage ended. I had no money for rent or bills, since all my savings had been used trying to keep my house and marriage. In desperation, I tried to go back to work. But, in no time, I was in so much pain; I left in tears and headed straight to the chiropractor's office. Because I had attempted to work—briefly—the insurance company refused to turn on my long-term disability coverage. I was left with the little money I had in my account, and no way to take care of myself and Sunny dog since my condition showed little improvement.

My pseudo-husband said he would help me if I rented us a two bedroom apartment. In an act of friendship and love, Kelsey said she wouldn't let me fall prey to his silver tongue or my heightened vulnerabilities. She flew out to California so she could drive Sunny and me back to her house to stay. As she was packing my possessions into my car, he skulked around watching or sitting on the couch, pouting. My little Kelsey might be half the size of him, and many inches smaller than me, but her bravery and strength towered over his cowardice. As we walked out the door for the last time, she stared him down.

He did not look back.

Where are we going?
Life as I knew it is gone,
far away from home.

Canyon Ferry Lake ice.
© *C.M. Arvish*

Mokuna 13: **Three Horse Town**

To handle the trip, I was drugged up and half-conscious, as the hours and miles rolled by, passing several state lines, delirious. In a partially lucid moment, I saw what I thought were large lawn ornaments or sculptures on the side of the road, only to realize they were bison grazing and relaxing in the warm grass.

Soon we came to a sign that read:

WELCOME TO MONTANA

Tumbleweeds, pine trees, and cottonwoods peppered the slow rolling beige hills, while creatures, looking as if they belonged in Africa, grazed alongside the cows and horses, in far stretching pasture lands.

"Those are cantaloupes," (antelopes) Kelsey joked.

Late in the day, we rolled into their three horse town, across a small cement bridge, and turned left at the grain silos that were edged by train tracks.

Kelsey and her husband had bought a two-story, three bedroom house, for $75,000 and were fixing it up. Lanky, somewhat warped windows ushered a soft dusty light onto the newly plastered, ochre-painted, walls. She described the thirteen layers of wallpaper and mortared lath they had laboriously removed. Then, she showed me part of the plastered wall, packed with horse hair from almost a hundred years ago.

Even with the interesting facts and impromptu house tour, I failed to see all its vintage charms through the sting of being ripped from my life, and the world I had worked so hard for. They were not set up for guests, but they did their best to make me comfortable.

In a matter of months, I had lost my marriage, my house, my good job, and was horribly injured. The devastation began to hit me, as I stared up at the cracked and peeling light blue ceiling, in an unfinished and unfurnished room, lying on their inflatable mattress in the corner, on the cold floor. I only had with me a few of my belongings in piles, and my clothes hastily shoved into garbage bags. But at least I had Sunny dog laying by my side and Kelsey downstairs.

Many nights, repressed pain and fear rose up from the depths of my subconscious and seeped out while I was trying to sleep, like to an irritating itch I couldn't scratch.

A panicked voice in my head was desperately yelling, "*Help me! Help me! Help me! Crap! Crap! Crap!*"

I rubbed my legs and hugged myself, trying to somehow calm whatever was expressing itself. Showers helped a little, if I was careful not to let the drops of hot water touch my left arm or hand. Slowly, the anguish somehow subsided enough for me to climb back in bed and drift off to sleep. This wretched state and intolerable feelings reared their ugly heads on and off for months, until the part of me trapped inside my body, full of misery, was finally able to let go.

I was used to a manicured California life, so I think I suffered from culture shock in this small Western town. It had a population of just under 2000 people, one grocery store, three bars, and three churches—perhaps locked in a race with each other for members.

There were odd sour smells coming from the walls and closets in Kelsey's house. Mice came and went freely in this hundred-plus-year-old home, right alongside the bats roosting in the attic. They mostly kept to themselves, but occasionally a bat swirled and swooped around the house to our screeches and laughter, while Kelsey's Border Collie Toby jumped up, snapping and leaping at the tiny creature.

With a white grocery bag and a flick of his wrist, her long-red-haired, rock and roll shirt wearing, Irish husband, saved us, and the wayward bat. Now, I like bats, but one flying around our heads in a confined space made us sound equivalent to giddy alarm bells, or gaily screeching banshees.

Kelsey did the laundry, made my bed, cooked, and helped me up and down her stairs.

I was able to slowly dress myself again, although hooking and unhooking a bra was out of the question with my bum left hand. Stretchy pants, over-sized tops, and pajamas became my outfits of necessity. I felt ashamed when I remembered "friends" in California speaking badly of Kelsey and her husband; calling them hippies, alternative, or throwbacks in time. Those same people called me once after my injury to see what had happened, and then cut me off completely, as if I was now tainted, bad luck, or being punished for some unknown wrong.

Without a second thought, Kelsey and Fred dropped everything and brought me into their home and lives. Our bonds grew; many days, she stayed at home taking care of me as I struggled to cope.

Both were patient with me, even if I tried to make dinner for them after they were gone all day, and they came home to squash, potatoes, or other weird and odd dishes. But at least watching movies with me was fun, if I wasn't hitting a wall or having a meltdown. With my memory now shot, it was like watching a brand new movie.

I HAD A QUICK referral to a surgeon in Great Falls, with a doctor who could not seem less interested in listening to me, unless I wanted a spinal fusion. I told him I definitely wanted the least invasive surgery I could find that would still help me. The surgeon became flippant and dismissive with me. He looked up slowly from his notes, and adjusted his glasses, saying, "I have done only a handful of less invasive micro-discectomies, but I could *try it*." This did not instill the greatest confidence in him.

So, my search continued.

Then, I received the letter. My leave without pay and employment had been terminated, and my medical coverage would end just a few days after receiving the notice. I raced out for a final MRI so I could have current films, then I was out of options.

Luckily, a chiropractor in Helena had a fantastic decompression machine from Australia. He was very knowledgeable, and he did as much as he could to help me. The machine slowly pulled some of the ruptured disc in while maintaining my internal structures, and gently increasing my range of motion. The more disc matter that was pulled in, the better my chances were at having a less invasive surgery. But, all of this treatment was paid for out-of-pocket. I only had enough money left in savings to pay for one or two more car payments, but not for ongoing, expensive medical care.

I resorted to repeatedly calling the corporate disability insurance carrier that had refused to turn on my long-term disability coverage, and demanded to speak to a manager, "I have already lost almost everything, and I am about to lose my car too!"

It took them four months to turn back on my coverage. They became a saving grace, and a thorn in my side, all at the same time.

I barely remember the first six months of being at Kelsey's. She said I was a miserable "witch," to be nice about it, and it took even longer for me to be able to walk Sunny dog without immediately turning back to her house in tears.

Maybe I had to almost die to be born anew. After being trapped in my body, wracked with pain for so long, once it started to subside a little, it was as if I had never heard a bird sing, seen a flower bloom before, or felt how soft my dog's ears were.

KELSEY WARNED ME with a smile of the twenty-below-zero winters, and the snow headed to Montana. I could hardly believe people survived the freezing temperatures she spoke of and didn't instantly perish as they walked to their cars in the morning. She and her husband spent most of their time in the winter far from town for his work, leaving Sunny and me to fend for ourselves.

We whiled away the days and weeks alone in their house, holed up for the winter. I piled on layers and layers of pajamas, socks, boots, and bathrobes.

"Quick, quick!" I said to Sunny dog as he raced out into the ice and snow-covered yard, back scrunched up in the cold, for his potty breaks. Condensation froze in my nostrils, and tiny airborne ice crystals lightly choked me with every shivering breath. The cold that seeped in, under the floorboards, from the dugout basement, was too much for the antiquated dinosaur of a furnace to combat.

Frigid air *constantly* blew in through the single-paned windows, over ice-encrusted sills. The bathroom and kitchen were barely insulated, giving me the experience of cooking and showering in an icebox. The small spray of lukewarm water, misting from the shower head, did little to thaw my hands and toes. When I complained about the pitifully lukewarm water, Kelsey did not believe me. Understandably so, after listening to me whine about my injuries for months and months.

Later, after the winter was over and they came back home, she took a shower and apologetically said, "Oops, you were right, one of the heating elements is out."

Sunny dog shivered in the night, so I started tucking him inside the covers with me, as I watched my breath fog in our room. I was glad for the fleece sheets, and down comforter, I had found, but the cold still managed to sneak its long bony fingers under our covers at night, as ice crystals crept silently around the window corners.

THE OWNER OF THE ranch, where Kelsey's husband Fred worked, flew back to his home in Alaska for the winter, leaving the entire ranch in their care. They had the run of the place. Some weekends, Sunny dog and I were able to visit, staying over in the huge, warm, cable-ready ranch home. The giant kitchen, soft beds, central heating, and hot water for showers, were a slice of heaven. We did not have cell phone service, but as spring started to roll around we were commonly jarred awake by the constant, warbled, squawky chatter of birds that looked like crows wearing dresses; magpies I was told. Along with these early morning visitors, the cedar waxwings arrived in softly peeping droves, happily devouring Mountain Ash berries, as families of crows curiously watched us on our rounds to the cattle pastures and chicken pen. Sunny was delighted when he found a baby fawn hiding in the woods on one of our walks, but we chased him away quickly, securing the safety of the small fragile deer.

Many mornings were spent chasing the surprisingly agile Scottish Highlander bull, and escape artist, away from the golf course portion of the ranch, and back into the main pasture and herd. Needless to say, bulls and golf courses don't mix. I watched as Kelsey, in muddy ranch boots, coaxed and herded the wily animal towards the wide open truck gate. But, the bull had other ideas. Standing next to the all too small human gate, looking sideways at Kelsey, he waited.

Reluctantly, and with a big sigh, she gave in. "You are such a weird bull!" she complained while unlatching the small gate, and stepping back. With horns far wider than the opening, I didn't see how he was going to fit. Then, he happily stepped forward, his massive head and horns cocked almost entirely sideways, as the red hairy beast moved daintily through the tiny gate, followed by our laughter.

The ranch was a welcome diversion from my suffering, but over the months of medical treatment and being mainly house-bound, a strange behavior started to appear with people who did not know me. I was a constant recipient of skepticism. I was trying as many traditional and non-traditional therapies that I could think of: acupuncture, naturopaths, herbal anti-inflammatories, you name it, while waiting for additional medical insurance or a payout from the lawsuit against the massage therapist. (The lawsuit was eventually fought off by the meanest, most ruthless female attorney I had ever had the bad luck of meeting. A couple of years after the lawsuit started, I settled for a small sum split with the medical insurance companies.)

Along with the difficulty of fighting for coverage, and the lawsuit, medical appointments became very stressful. Some doctors greeted me curtly, half-listening dismissively, as they rolled their eyes, or met my gaze with raised eyebrows, as I described my symptoms.

I could not understand being confronted with their jadedness and reluctance to help me. Having been raised as an extremely trustworthy and honest person, this was hard to bear. I did not choose or cause my injury. It was violently forced upon me, without mercy or regard to my personal goals and wishes. Now, many strangers began treating me as if I was a villain, except, thankfully, the people closest to me who had known me for years. I wished naysayers could see my heart, and know that what I was telling them was true. But, I realized, some people have predetermined mindsets that are hard to change. So, I stopped trying.

Ironically, I guarded the auto insurance company I worked for from false claims, and have been trusted in my life to watch children, animals, and the elderly. Now, I was left begging and fighting big nasty companies for coverage so I could survive. For someone whose mind shut down, and whose speech slurred due to the exhaustion and pain from even the most trivial of daily tasks—confronting and fighting insurance companies, was a monumental undertaking. It was difficult trying to heal myself under an air of mistrust, so thick it made my skin crawl.

So, I was petrified to meet the official medical examiner on our appointed date and time. He held in his hands the means to leave me in devastation, or to authorize medical coverage that could eventually lead to surgery. To my great relief, he understood exactly what had happened to me, and what I was going through, and agreed wholeheartedly that not accepting a fusion and going with decompression, even though it was slow, was the better way to go.

As I recounted what had happened to me, he even made a joke. "Yea, though I walk through the valley of the shadow of death, I will not buy a condo there."

I was notified by mail that my medical coverage would come online in a year, but in the meantime, I lived under an uncomfortable cloud of scrutiny. Neighbors became increasingly bold in their pushy, disrespectful questioning; becoming self-appointed interrogators: "So, you don't work? Why aren't you trying to work? You don't look injured," they spewed.

I USED TO take great offense at people trying to help me land my kayak or open a door for me. "I can do it myself," I told them.

It was common for me to head out, ecstatic, into the open ocean amid storms, wind, and waves, loving every hectic minute of it, almost impervious to the wet and cold.

I told a woman that I used to kayak, horseback ride, rappel into caves, do half-triathlons, scuba dive, etc. and was met with a bewildered look of shock on her face, "You?!"

As if she thought I *liked* to sit around all day recuperating *just* for the fun of it. Quite the *opposite* was true. I intensely wanted to do all I used to do, and more. Slowly, I learned to have cowhide thick skin, and focus on the people close to me who mattered most in my life.

MANY DAYS, AS SUNNY and I returned to the car after a pleasant and healing walk in the woods, I felt the weight of someone's stare, only to shift my gaze to a person hurriedly writing notes on a clipboard in a non-descript car, with their card-badge lying on the dashboard, face down. How creepy it was to be followed and peered at by the "lurkers," as I called them. They popped up in countless places: the grocery store, medical offices, but *especially* at trailheads. I don't know what they wanted to see as I walked slowly with Sunny dog, but someone seemed interested.

They thought they were so sneaky, but some were as covert as a tsunami alarm test blaring, as my sister and I had swum in the pristine waters off of Lanikai beach.

While swimming, and trying to ignore the post-world-war-two sirens, we enjoyed a favorite pastime of googly-eyed, baby-puffer-fish spotting. Or, there was the endless enjoyment I received watching a baby crab feverishly swim after my sister, desperately trying to cling to her swimsuit for safety, as she ran in slow motion, arms in drastic swoops, making squeaks and shrieks, trying to flee her white-and-beige-speckled one-inch foe.

Sometimes, they would catch her, so with tears in my eyes from laughing so hard, I had to be the brave one, and detach the sweet innocent little thing turned perceived monster, saving it from her fear-fueled wrath. Ironically, I wouldn't have minded letting one hide on me, safe from being eaten by a fish while we swam. But of course, and without fail, they always bypassed me and headed straight for her.

We usually had fun despite all the racket, but other intrusions are harder to ignore.

One such incident took place on a balmy afternoon, as Sunny dog and I meandered up a gently curving, pine-needle-cushioned trail in Helena, Montana. I'm sure the man thought he was one of the stealthy ones, until I felt his absolute voyeuristic elation hit me like an arrow on my left side. Turning quickly, I saw him on a small bluff next to me hunched down, small handheld camera pointed right at me.

Seeing I had caught him, he turned on his heels and tried to casually walk away. When I returned to the trailhead, the only other car was a beat-up red SUV of some type, its scratched vanity plate read: I VIDEO. *Smooth.*

He must be a "lurker," or have a very odd habit, I thought. If I was still running around naked in forests I could understand, but at this point in my life, I had taken to hiking fully clothed.

Well, most of the time. There was that one day in Auburn, California. But *that's* a different story.

Never knowing if, or when, another "lurker" might pop up, one cold, winter day I was especially glad to have my all wheel drive Subaru Forester after being followed turn-by-turn as I drove easily up an icy, snow-filled canyon. When the car behind me foundered on the ice, I looked back to see a pouting woman look on as I drove away deep into the mountains.

For the first time in a long time, our surroundings were truly peaceful, as we walked in the remote and swirling idyllic snow globe scenery. Sunny ran and played, decked out in the blue and red plaid fleece snow coat and boots he was so proud of. I was enormously relieved not to have someone peering at me in the woods, for once.

I understood after working for a large insurance company that requesting surveillance on claimants was commonplace during any medical case, so we could "check up" on the injured. But to have it turned around on me was strange and unnerving, even if they were just doing their jobs.

I hoped it wasn't some type of twisted karma in which I had to learn how it felt firsthand. In some way, I just hoped "they" were going to be happy I was trying to get out and build some more stamina, movement, and joy, and stop stalking me. Dealing with all the "lurkers" made me long for "my hike" in the tropical mountains near Manoa, where peace and the love of the ancestors surrounded me. But, as I ventured further out into the forests of Montana, the wild and open spaces started slowly healing my heart.

I had lost almost everything, but in return, I had gained some of my life's real treasures: my friends and family, and the sweetest dog I have ever known.

I STILL BECOME downhearted and pouty inside when I think of all the activities I cannot do. Then, I delight in watching Sunny dog walking with me in the beautiful forests of the biggest dog park in the world called Montana. With a myriad of wildflowers poking their tiny heads through the windswept grasses, as he chased squirrels and chipmunks with a giant smile on his face, I started to notice some happiness growing inside me.

God knew to bring me to Montana, to the bosom of these mountains, to hide and heal me, so I could find myself again, in a truer and more sincere way.

So, I was relieved when one night over the phone Fred told my not-quite-husband back in California that if he stepped foot in Montana to find me, he'd have to face Fred's shotgun.

Kelsey and Fred had taken care of me for over a year. We had some fun times despite my issues and even spent occasional hot summer days floating in the lake near their house. But eventually, they grew weary of me staying with them. With my enchanting, cheery personality, surrounded by an aura of Snow White, how could they become tired of me? Well, there's a limit, for even the most charitable of people. It was time for me to go.

On one of our many, winter, wondering days.

© C.M. Arvish

Hobo Spider
(*Eratigena agrestis*, formerly
Tegenaria agrestis &
Pleasedon'thitemeopsis)

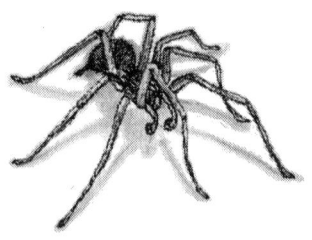

Mokuna 14: **Pixie-Haired Monster and the Lovely Red House**

Why I sometimes have the worst radar for mean, horrible, people, I will never know. Maybe I had to meet her so I could find where my strength was hiding, and learn to stand up for myself again. I met Kelsey's neighbor woman innocently enough, as we went together on trips to town, perusing material stores and craft shops. She took me to her Reiki groups, filled with enlightened, pleasant people, who reminded me of my mom and her spiritual groups of friends. We took turns giving and receiving the gift of Reiki to each other, amidst fragrant candlelight and softly playing music.

Since we seemed to have some connections, I asked her if she had a room to rent. She enthusiastically said yes.

I shouldn't have let her cute pixie haircut and Betty Homemaker look fool me, but I couldn't see past her amiable exterior.

The day we moved my small amount of belongings and a futon mattress over to her house, she said she changed her mind about renting me the room, but she had her covered porch available. Since it was too late to go back to Kelsey and Fred's, and I needed a place for us to stay, I agreed. She put an old scratched dresser and bookshelves up next to the sliding glass door to divide the room, my futon on the floor, some dusty old ratty orange curtains up next to three splintered raw-wood bookshelves, and that was it.

Soon, she turned into a nasty, monstrous woman, badgering her husband and me as she nitpicked every move we made in "her house." I was allowed one drawer in the refrigerator and if I placed food elsewhere, she shoved it back in the drawer, almost smashing it, and then enjoyed staring at me, waiting for a response. I, who almost never argued and avoided conflict like the plague, had this woman try to pick fights with me about nonsensical, insane issues. Like how a sponge should be used, if the fan was left on in the bathroom, or if it wasn't. I told her that with my damaged neck and weak arms, I couldn't fix the screen door when it fell off the runners, but she would hear none of it, fiercely yelling at me when I could not re-hang it properly. I couldn't even wash the dishes correctly in her eyes, so I was given one spoon, one fork, and one knife—from the old set—along with a small outdated bowl and plate to hand wash in the half bathroom and leave to dry on a tattered yellow towel behind the toilet. I started avoiding her whenever possible, walking on egg-shells, trying to guess what she wanted, or what would set her off next.

ON HER OCCASIONAL nice days, she wanted to sew with me—big mistake! Any small error, in her eyes, and she flew off the handle, exclaiming how abusive and mean I was. Even the smallest of rebuttals infuriated her. So, skirting her invitations became a survival tactic. As a good natured person, yet injured, and confused, I hardly had the energy for her confrontations. Some days, Sunny and I snuck out the back when she wasn't looking. One of the benefits of avoiding the "pixie-haired monster" was finding little Gems in Townsend such as the bakery, a glass blowing place, an eclectic craft store, and a quilt shop. We also found, just down the road, large ponds on Canyon Ferry Lake, which were overburdened by swans, geese, fish, and the occasional moose, happily munching on vegetation. Our little outings were a much needed respite, but the rest of the time, I stayed in my little area, quietly hiding under the covers and holding Sunny dog, as she yelled at me across the "divider."

I started to see a pattern. She was resentful and abusive and loved to pick fights, but when a person eventually stood up to her or fought back, she played the victim, accusing *them* of being abusive. I began standing up to her, which *really* pissed her off. I stood my ground and calmly looked at her, while shaking in my boots, telling her *exactly* what I thought of her and how she had no right to treat me, or anyone else, like that and that *she* was the abusive one.

"I am not very *pleased* with you!" She retorted, scurrying like a snarling weasel out of the room, but she started to leave me alone.

After renting from her through summer and learning how to stand up for myself, I went back to Kelsey's with my tail between my legs and a time limit for finding another place that Sunny and I could call home.

I searched the internet for a place in Helena that I could afford on my meager monthly stipend, and for a landlord who somehow wouldn't mind my now destroyed credit rating and a broken lease in California. That could be a tall order.

By the grace of God, I found a pleasant little apartment in a huge red Victorian house, in close proximity to the cobble-stoned walking mall and cafés. I met the owner of the house, gave him a check for my deposit, and that was it. He didn't bat an eye and there was even a nice yard outside for Sunny, not to mention the miles of trails we found, just up the road from our new home.

It was a small, nice, and clean apartment, with lanky bay windows that let in ample light, giving the space an airy feel. There was a pass-through bedroom and closet that led to the cutest little café kitchen, painted in cheery red with a wall-mounted table nestled inside bay windows. The table was just perfect for some calico linens I had found at a local antique store.

I decorated with yellow-and-white-striped, French-styled, café curtains, and a vase of flowers.

The bathroom was not a full bath, but was more akin to an old-fashioned water closet. I didn't mind, it had warm water.

Our new home was a small and humble place with a few more spiders than I liked, but it was ours. There was no one yelling at us, no one threatening us, and we were not intruding on others' privacy. It was ours, and with another winter coming on, the gas fireplace heater was a Godsend, comfortingly popping on to warm us, as reflections of orange and yellow flames danced off the walls and antique moldings. I remember waking up in the night, lying there holding Sunny dog under the covers, watching the flames and being so thankful. For the first time, it was a joy to see the snow arrive.

SOON AFTER WE MOVED in, an issue arose that threatened to tear Kelsey and me apart for the first time, in our twenty-year-plus friendship. She asked, while I was staying at her house overnight, if Fred would be allowed to sleep at my apartment after he had been out partying all night with his friends. I had no leg to stand on, or right to complain, while they were taking care of me. But, now I had my own place. My memories harkened back to the days of my dad's bar, after a big party and before the cleaning crew came in. The reek of stale alcohol, cigarettes—and if it were a super special night—maybe some vomit tidbits out back, made me cringe. The vivid past recollection of that appetizing potpourri possibly lingering in my apartment, and especially my bed, disgusted me, causing serious pause. Add to that, my inability to clean properly, and not wanting someone, anyone, in my special space.

Turning slowly toward her with the office chair squeaking, I sheepishly said "no," trying quickly to explain why he couldn't stay in my apartment and rattling off my excuses.

Her eyebrows raised in surprise.

I swiveled back around to face the computer, *gulp.*

She became silent, like just before a storm, as the air filled with her anger.

"I need you to leave," she demanded.

I slinked out of her house, Sunny at my heels, relieved to be in my car and away from the hurricane's path. She may be small, but she can be as intimidating as a rabid Chihuahua.

She refused to speak to me for months, and then finally, she sent me an e-mail, and wrote, "After *all* we did for you, and took care of you for so long, *how* could you do that to Fred?"

I had set a boundary for my new place and did not want it disrupted, but I could see her point, and apologized. I told her how grateful I was for them, but that I had to stand up and not allow any potentially odious person in my apartment. She did not respond.

A THERAPIST I SAW at the time, said to let myself cry. I was reluctant, not thinking I needed to. In the mountains the next day with Sunny and the quiet forest all around us, I suddenly started to cry so hard I doubled over, unable to continue walking, or standing, as wrenching sobs and clenched muscles gripped my body, beyond my conscious control as the primitive depths of despair clawed their way out. I thought it would never end, as tears flowed relentlessly out of my eyes. Then, very slowly and to my surprise, as I sat against a sturdy pine tree, breathing and blinking away my tears, looking over the trees and houses far below, my crying ended. I never cried over my now ex-husband, or the loss of my old life again.

There was a song playing in my car soon after that, which especially resonated with me, and one of the lines went a little like this. Let the old life fade away, and let this new life be your saving grace. (Jeremy Camp's, "*Let it Fade*").

I let those words sink into my soul, as the days passed waiting for my medical coverage to begin. I found the nearby local library and buried my nose in spiritual and goddess books. I searched for the balance of men and women in a patriarchal society, and for what had given me such strength and joy in my youth. Books like Margaret Starbird's, *The Woman with the Alabaster Jar,* and Sylvia Browne's, *The Mystical Life of Jesus: An Uncommon Perspective on the Life of Christ,* along with the time-worn, soft, and fragrant pages of Jean Markale's, *The Great Goddess: Reverence of the Divine Feminine from the Paleolithic to the Present.* My kind and wise mom also sent a handsome red and black book on the I Ching, along with *Amulets of the Goddess: Oracle of Ancient Wisdom,* by Nancy Blair, for me to peruse.

The knowledge in these and other books was bolstering. As some peace and comfort was starting to burgeon into my life again, a daily prayer formed in my mind that made sense to me. I thanked the female and male aspects of God, and asked for protection, peace, light, and the love of God to surround us: my friends, my family, and the Earth. Angel trinkets, wind chimes, natural objects, sage, and holy water, became commonplace in my apartment.

Around the same time frame, I was introduced, in the dream world, to what I suspect was a spirit guide of mine. She seemed to be an auntie, from my dad's side of the family, wearing a monochromatic ecru tunic and short pants, with close-cut light brown hair. She appeared dressed in all of the same soft tones, except for her beautiful bright blue eyes. She came to teach me lessons in a series of four dreams.

In the first dream, I was swimming alone in front of my grandpa Bill's house, when all of a sudden, an enormous four-story wave reared up in an imposing posture, threatening to engulf me. I was terrified and unable to flee. A split-second before the raging water crashed on top of my head, destroying me, I woke up, startled and shaken.

The next night the dream started out the same way. To my horror, the cold, dark, wave rose up again in front of me, without warning, edging closer and closer. Again, I was powerless and terrified. Then, I heard my newly revealed spirit guide suggest softly, "Say, Jesus." Since I had not been raised with his name as commonplace, combined with several insincere occurrences at a couple of churches; it came as a strange suggestion. The wave was almost ready to engulf me. Taking her advice, I cried out one word—Jesus! Like a miracle, the wave disappeared, leaving me happy, safe, and relieved, in calm, beautiful, flat water. Having learned this simple and powerful lesson, the dreams stopped for a while.

Months later, I found myself in another deep sleep. In the dream, I awoke in a dark room with no windows. To the left of the metal-framed bed, made up with one pillow, a sheet, and a thin, tattered quilt, was a wooden bedside table, and small black lamp, barely giving off any light. In a split-second, an evil, menacing demon appeared only a few feet away, hovering in the corner. Sitting straight up in bed, my face turned sharply towards the threat, horrified and barely able to speak. I was frozen in fear. This time, I knew what to do. With barely a breath in my chest, one desperate word escaped from my lips—Jesus. To my great relief, poof, the demon disappeared, leaving me safe, and filled with joy.

Sometime later, came my fourth and favorite dream. This time there was no fear, no terror, no threat, instead it gave me an enduring impression that has stuck with to this day and every day from there on out. It was me and Jesus in the desert, sitting on a large, pale, cream-colored rock, overlooking the arid landscape. Sometimes my head was on his shoulder and other times we sat next to each other, laughing or engaging in light banter about nothing in particular, as if he was my best friend. There was no condemnation, no falseness, just joy, the gorgeous desert landscape, and Jesus. I didn't have to be perfect, or skinny, or drive a fancy car, or wear fake eyelashes. There was no judgment. Who I was, with a sincere heart, was all I needed to receive love, grace, protection, and the new joy I needed to lift me up and set me free again.

I don't tell very many people this, but I now consider myself a hippy, nature-loving, tree-hugging, eclectic, adventurous, crazy artist, and a closet Jesus freak. My church is in the mountains and I see God in a snowflake.

Now, whenever I am scared or need to call in white light all around me, I say to myself, "White light Jesus." To me, it seems, when I am cloaked in his light, darkness or evil cannot see or find me. I also incorporate, or "call in" the powerful energies of Mary one, Mary two, the female aspect of God, nature spirits, and angels in all their glory. So, when I have no Idea what to do, or what to say, I can always blurt out, "White light Jesus," to any negativity, nightmare, or to an intimidating semi truck passing on the highway that freaks me out. And if someone comes at me aggressively or with ill-intent, I *might* just throw a silent "White light Jesus" their way, just for good measure.

I was starting to feel safer and more secure in our lovely red house, but missed my goofy family in Hawaii and the ever-lapping waves of the tropical seashore. A trip to the islands was in order.

I FLEW TO HAWAII for a quick vacation with my dad and stepmom before I was snowed in for the winter. The mellow and rainy visit was almost done, but I still had a strong desire to make the pilgrimage up my trail, even in my condition. My flight back to the mainland was leaving in five hours, so we rushed up the steep neighborhood roads and parked alone at the head of the trail. The muddy ground was wet and slippery, too treacherous for my dad, so he decided to wait by the car, staying near enough to make sure I came back okay. After carefully stepping on roots and rocks, the mud became too thick to continue, so, I only made it as far as the tall, fragrant pines near the upper entry point. I decided to lean against one of them, arm lazily wrapped around the trunk, rough curly bark scratching my cheek, slightly rocking side to side, while wind played amongst its highest branches. The eerie creaking of trees rubbing together was the only sound as I quietly watched slowly crawling rain clouds curve in and out of the mist-fringed mountains, one last time.

All of a sudden, I heard in my left ear, "Ala ke kua" loud enough to startle me and I exclaimed aloud, "Ala ke kua, what is that!?"

The image of a half Hawaiian, half Caucasian, (hapa), woman's face, leaning towards my ear, was left etched in my mind. She had fluffy, brown, shoulder length hair, and a pleasant smile.

Knowing there was a time limit, and that my dad was waiting patiently by the car, I didn't stop to let the message sink in but was elated with it as I slowly made my way back down the precarious trail.

Without "my hike" as an option, we headed to the upper end of Mānoa Valley and the glorious Lyon Arboretum. The gorgeous grounds never seem to grow old, and with my dad's extensive knowledge of the tropics, and my endless fascination with all the colors, textures, and plants in the park, we had a jolly, soggy time before rushing back to their house.

I did not have a chance to look up the translation, as we devoured dinner quickly and dashed off to the airport. Upon landing in Montana, the contrast between the vertical green jungles I had just left in the Arboretum and the beige-ish, white, horizontal landscape I looked out on, was dramatic.

The next day, at the local library, I used one of their computers and looked up the disembodied message. It meant, "The pathway of God," or "Pathway of the Gods." It surprised and humbled me, knowing I had never heard that saying before and that I could not have made it up. I was very thankful for that message and the surreal way it had been delivered.

From that day forward, my prayers ended with, "Mahalo, ke ala ke kua. Thank you, the pathway of God."

THAT CHRISTMAS, I WAS surprised by my family, with the gift of a used laptop computer, so I could communicate with them more often and not feel so alone. I signed up quickly for the common social media sites and indulged in some online TV series.

I don't know what compelled me to have the crazy idea to fill out an online dating site's profile, but I did. Since I hadn't even had surgery yet, there was no way I was in any shape to date. I kept telling myself that I was just seeing what type of men were around places I was thinking of moving, like, Ashland, Oregon, or Albuquerque, New Mexico. Just for kicks and giggles, I peeked at men in Montana. But, I believed that only cowboys, and people I wouldn't have much in common with, lived in this state.

Little did I know who would come into my life.

Flowers and pine cones,
far stretching mountains and clouds,
is my new home here?

Balsam Arrowroot flowers carpet Montana's
mountainsides in the springtime.

Mokuna 15: **Tupelo Honey**

I slipped my e-mail, to the kind-eyed teacher, on the last day of my three-month free trial. We had both been very honest with our profiles, and after connecting through the anonymous dating site, we wanted to get to know each other better. As the days passed, we enjoyed exchanging e-mails with each other, and learning details about our lives and personalities. But, in the back of my mind, I knew I had a secret. Once I told him about my injury and pending surgery, I was sure he would be scared away.

Sitting in my blue and gray thrift store office chair in front of my laptop, I dreaded opening my inbox, knowing I would have to read his response. Then, I saw words I could not have imagined rolling off the page, as I nervously read on. He said no, he was not scared away, and he had been terribly injured and disabled for a year himself, so he knew exactly what I was going through. I was so happy and relieved. After that, I was finally brave enough to start texting him.

I had just met a cultured, well-educated teacher, who was a theater actor, radio DJ for MTPR (Montana Public Radio), and he loved to cook foods from around the world. I have to admit, he blew all my preconceived notions about Montana men out of the water. He was not a cowboy, a hick, or a redneck. He was also a non-smoker, and non-drinker. Additionally, even in this land locked-state, he was a water-baby like me—relishing the times he spent on the Oregon and Washington coasts as a young man.

Several weeks later, and after listening to his soft velvet voice permeating my tiny apartment during his *What I Like About Jazz* radio show, I plucked up my courage to call him. We talked for hours that first night. (Show times and information are listed in the back of the book).

I didn't ask for this wonderful man to come into my life, but was he delivered to my doorstep, in a big red bow.

AT THE SAME TIME, Kelsey decided she still loved me. I was so happy we were communicating again. I couldn't have imagined living the rest of my life without her. Ironically, she later thanked me for our fight. If I had not refused to allow her husband to stay in my apartment, she may not have been spurred to briefly leave him, find herself again, and repair parts of her marriage that needed binding. We laughed together later, because I might not have met John either, if we had not temporarily parted ways.

FINALLY, IT WAS TIME to meet in person. I drove two hours over a mountain pass, along a winding river, and below dappled clouds floating through warm sunny skies, while butterflies spun around my belly wildly.

On my car radio, there was a woman with a gorgeous voice (later I found out she was Cassandra Wilson) singing a beautiful song I had never heard before about Tupelo honey. Sunny dog and I arrived in Missoula, so I took a deep breath, and pulled into his driveway. There he was, with his welcoming smile, and kind green eyes looking back at me. Sunny ran up to him as we embraced in our very first hug. Later that evening, he played me one of his favorite songs. You guessed it. "Tupelo Honey" by Van Morrison, rang out from the stereo. "It's that song!" I said, happily surprised for the coincidence.

On our first weekend together, he took me to the Missoula, Jazzoula festival. He knew many of the musicians from his years being the stage manager and assistant soundman, and was commended for the great resonance he helped produce in concert with the players. While he was busy back on the soundboard, I wandered into the neighboring nave of St. Anthony's Church, lured by the singing of the Dolce Canto choir, who sounded like a chorus of angels. I listened breathlessly to the glorious choir practice for a long time, before returning to the adjoining building, where the Jazz musicians played on into the night.

A cute, funny, little gray-haired woman sat next to me. We chatted and joked, becoming fast friends. I asked her what her name was. She turned to me, looking straight into my eyes, and said, "Hope."

I was momentarily surprised at her inspirational name, but held the mist back from my eyes, since I was in a crowded room full of people. We continued our occasional laughing and banter while listening to the swinging music.

She left the show before me, and I almost wondered if I had been sitting next to an angel that night.

I returned the next weekend, and the next. The days were mixed together between warm cuddles at night, and following him around during the day. I accompanied him to the Missoula Children's Theatre to see dance recitals, and into the secret room where he ran his radio show. I even helped out with the theater camp kids, as they learned in their classes.

Sunny dog took to John right away, unlike the common cowering that took place with my ex. John told me, excitedly, that his favorite dog from many years ago was also named Sunny, and that she had the same forehead, and look in her eyes. Maybe a reincarnation, to be with both of us, we jested.

I stayed one weekend with John, at the MCT camp on Flathead Lake that he helped to manage. The joy, from the gangs of extremely extroverted, high-energy, kids, singing and dancing, was contagious.

The camp was set on a crystal clear lake, rimmed with large sparkly granite rocks, scraggly wind-blown trees, and rolling hills.

Just offshore, soft, gray, and white osprey hovered soundlessly, almost floating over the glassy lake water, until they spied a fish, then swiftly dove, and hit the lake with a loud splash. Catch in claw, heavy with wet wings, they rose back into the air, only stopping momentarily in mid-flight to shake off the water. Back they flew, with the fish still wiggling in their talons, to cute little fuzzy babies, with eager hungry bellies, hidden in nests like tree earrings.

John had lived in Montana almost his entire life. After meeting many of his longtime friends, and seeing how he was trusted as a teacher, and camp director, I started to be a bit more confident. Even if I did not trust myself to be the best judge of character, so many people around him did, and told me what a good, trustworthy, loyal, and wonderful man he was.

I asked him if he was worried about me being a gypsy-hearted, wild-spirited woman, and I will never forget what he said. "Go where you want to go, do what you want to do, just come back to me." He knew the best way to keep a wild animal, was to set it free.

Sunny was falling in love with him too, so as the weeks, and then months went by, it became harder and harder to drive back to Helena after our weekends together.

BEFORE JOHN AND I had met, Kelsey and I were floating in the Canyon Ferry Lake one day. I was still confused about if it was right to leave he-who-shall-not-be-named or not—If you can believe that—and in her ever wise, and helpful way she said, "What if you went back to that horrible man, and never meet the sweet man that you are supposed to be with, the one who is meant for you?" I now thanked her over and over again for being right. With teasing laughter, and a side smirk, she responded, "Of *course* I was right, I told you so."

FALL WAS COMING, the leaves were turning, and with the risk of being trapped on the other side of a snow-covered pass, we decided I shouldn't leave anymore.

So, his sassy, funny, sister Gina and her husband helped, "Pack me up, move me out, *rawhide!*" It must be a Montana thing.

As we settled into John's home, I loved watching Sunny relish his new backyard. He stuck his nose in the grass, and then flopped onto to one side in a fit of pure joy, rolling, and twisting his body, groaning with pleasure in the sunshine.

Missoula sits inside a bowl of snow-swirled, halva like mountains, divided by many robust rivers, with long hiking trails leading up and away from the town in several directions. There are theaters, art, a college, great restaurants, a sprawling outdoor market, and just enough of a nature-loving, eclectic clothes-wearing, vintage bike-riding, organic garden-growing, hippy-minded people presence, to make me feel welcomed.

Of course, Sunny was pleased with the area too. After a short drive, we could be deep in the forest, practically alone.

Under a thick cover of tree-studded grasslands, the warmth of spring and summer unleashes a cornucopia of brightly patterned butterflies, blown in with the breezes, to feed on a riot of wildflowers carpeting the ground.

Elegant, almost weightless white butterflies, with gray, speckled, tissue-paper-thin wings, floated in circles high above in the pine boughs, while chubby, fuzzy, bumblebees made frantic, buzzing noises, and zigzagged erratically below.

If the forest nymphs favor you, a bright green bee, no bigger than a pinky nail, might briefly show itself rummaging in the center of a flower for pollen, reflecting a shiny beetle shell, glinting like a moving jewel, with tiny iridescent wings.

Grasshoppers pop into the air unexpectedly, snapping and clicking their frantic retreats. Yellow-breasted meadowlarks arrive, their songs ringing out across fields from their perches on the tippy tops of loan trees, amplifying their songs perfectly. Male Mountain Bluebirds flash their brilliance in the sunlight, and catch one of those grasshoppers that happen to pop in just the "right" direction.

Occasionally, voices emerge somewhere in the woods, laughing and talking, only to recede again, leaving us with the soft happy peeps and chirps of tiny birds searching for food.

Wind carrying the scent of honey, vanilla, and damp earth quietly sighs ever so lightly through the pine needles and grasses, only broken by sudden whistling wing beats, rapid beak castanets, or raven caws.

Sunny loves chasing squirrels of course, and luckily they are far too fast, to ever be caught, but this doesn't make the game any less thrilling for him, and we have a good arrangement; he doesn't eat my chocolate, and I don't eat his deer poop.

As fall rolls around, tall stately Tamarack trees glow gold and orange like living embers above burgundy, olive tapenade-tinted leaves, and wheat cracker-colored underbrush. Leaves shiver slightly, falling as we pass, crunching under our feet. There is a chill in the air, a soft scarf around my face, and bright white snowberries peppering the forest. Arrow-head points of geese trumpet their departure through darkening skies. All clear signs of the changing seasons.

When the snow finally falls, clinging to branches like sparkling, white, downy pillows, perfectly decorating the winter wonderland around us, Sunny and I wander up into the hills, before returning chilled, back to John's warm, safe, hugs. We are a good eight hours from the ocean, but in times like these, I don't miss it so much.

It felt safe and snug sharing a home with John. We cooked all sorts of great foods, listened to his large collection of music, and watched movies together. At night, we climbed into bed with Sunny, and his large black kitty curled up next to us. Even simple days just being together and hanging out felt nice. He liked my artsy, colorful, sometimes weird personality. And I am happy to announce that he hasn't tried even once to dominate, manipulate, or oppress me—a refreshing fact, after the years dealing with he-who-shall-not-be-named. We frequented cafés together, drank some of the best locally roasted fresh coffee from Black Coffee Roasting Company, headed out on road trips, went camping, or met up with friends for dinner and a game night. He had to help me with many daily tasks, but he didn't seem to mind.

The next hurdle we had to overcome was my surgery, but he said we would face it together.

He held my life
in his hands

John and Sunny dog.
© *C.M. Arvish*

Mokuna 16: **Frankenstein Holes and A Frog Fish**

My chiropractor, bedecked with his Einstein look-alike hair-do, and fatherly kind countenance, was ever ready to listen, and always there to help go to bat for me against one-eyed, goliath, insurance companies. He worked hard, preparing me for the upcoming event.

That morning, as we waited patiently for my scheduled surgery time, John distracted me with lighthearted jokes, and teasing. Then, suddenly, several nurses came in the room with a flurry of activity. Efficiently rushing around, one said, "There has been a cancellation, we are getting you ready for the operating room very quickly."

Then, a man appeared, describing the pick line that was to be inserted from my neck to my heart. He said the procedure was dangerous, but he was going to "*watch* me carefully."

I had no time to react or respond.

John kissed my forehead. "I love you," he said, and held my hand until they wheeled me away.

It was so frightening, putting my life, and body, in someone else's hands; I did not know if, or how, I would wake up. I just had to let go, as the anesthesia took effect.

I CAME TO in a dimly lit room, in a great deal of pain, and unable to move very much. John and my mom were there by my side, and I was so happy to be alive, and not paralyzed. I had made it through, now I just had to heal—again.

Every noise and bright light was intolerable. I had been cut from the middle of my neck, to in-between my shoulder blades. Since the rupture was at an odd angle, the surgeon had to cut through many layers of muscle while opening me up, and then he had to sew all the delicate tissues back together again.

In my hospital bed, I focused on being calm and extremely patient, as I waited to be released. I had no choice. While dealing with my horrible injury, and the aftermath, I learned (by default) to have a lot of patience and perseverance.

One morning, I had to tinkle so badly but couldn't get out of bed. A nurse came in my room to help, but she did not center the bowl under my rear properly, so I accidentally wet both myself and the mattress.

They had to change the sheets with me in the bed. As they tilted my body to one side, a nurse dug her fingers right in the middle of the slice down my neck. I sobbed in agony, trembling as they sheepishly finished their task. I was left shaking in pain and shock. It took all I had inside of me to calm down again, once they left.

Finally, back at home, days and days later, I was sitting up at the dining room table. In a confused mental state, and probably on too many painkillers, a terrifying thought washed over me. *Had I been sent back in time somehow, to start the torture all over again? I feared this was the beginning of the injury and not the after surgery pain and healing process supposed to help alleviate my symptoms.* It was unnerving, because I was going to have to wait several long months to find out if having the surgery had been the right choice or not. I had no way of knowing, at that point, what would become of me.

As I started the slow process of healing, we made light of my "Frankenstein screw holes," the dents that were left in my scalp from being securely affixed to the surgical chair.

Once again, I had to be taken care of like a baby as they washed me, dressed me, and cooked all of my meals. Several months went by before I could lift my arms up past my chin and delicately shower myself. Lying flat in bed was not an option, so we bought a bed wedge. I felt like a mummy, propped up, neck brace on, holding myself stiff as a board to avoid the slightest twist or movement. Cuddling at night was exchanged for only the tips of my fingers being able to reach one of John's arms or Sunny's side. Luckily, we were fully stocked with movies and music since I was basically house-bound.

Taxi cabs eventually took me to surgery follow-ups, but they were oblivious of my neck brace and whipped around slow cars through puddles or slammed on brakes, leaving me in tears and the driver apologetic. I couldn't stand for any length of time and stepping wrong on the ground shot pain up and down my spine. Instead of a strong Amazonian-like woman, I felt like a powder puff.

I wore a neck brace for six months, and couldn't drive for nine. But, in the middle of all this, came an exciting and thoughtful gift from John of a tabletop easel, new brushes, and paint. Very carefully, and with patience, I was finally able to return to one of my great loves, painting. (To see artwork, go to, www.redbubble.com/people/cmarvishart)

WE HAD BOUGHT our tickets to Hawaii long before the surgery, thinking it would be very healing and fun for us to meet up with my dad, stepmom, sister, brother, and his girlfriend for a family week in the islands.

The surgery had been delayed for three months, and six weeks is barely enough time to be moving around much after a major spinal surgery, let alone to be able to travel. So, with our flight waiting, we loaded me up with pain meds, and headed on our way.

Sitting up on an airplane, in a neck brace, for hours away from my bed and memory foam was a struggle, to say the least.

When we finally arrived, I went straight to bed. I was so happy lying there, with the balmy trade winds rattling the Lychee tree leaves, softly wafting in through the windows and across my body. Geckos clicked, and waggled up the walls and window frames, as my family talked and laughed with each other in the other room.

Even though it was difficult to be away from home, the trip was so good for my soul. We giggled as John wrestled with my bathing suit, since he was assigned the fun task of pulling it up, and up, and up, while I held onto my neck brace with one hand, and the wall with the other.

Most mornings I woke up feeling like a ton of bricks, all stiff and gnarly. So, my family took me gingerly with them to the ocean for a morning "swim." After carefully assisting me down the slippery steps in front of the Elk's Club, and into the water, they went off on their own swimming adventures, leaving me to float, which was fine with me.

I floated face down, with a snorkel and mask on, doing my best impression of a storm weathered log, or detritus, just allowing the ocean to hold my whole body. It was really the only place I could relax *a* little. As I floated in the shallows over the white sand and coral, watching sunlight shimmer and dance in ribbons below me, curious fish inspected this new object floating above their homes.

To me, it felt like being held in the hands of God as I was cupped gently in the water. One of the best parts of being such a passive snorkeler, for the first time in my life, was noticing a very rare and shy fish. I couldn't wait to tell my dad that I had hovered over a Hawaiian frogfish for a long time, while he eyeballed me back through his spongy beige exterior, blending in expertly to the reef.

Startled, and excited, dad said he had not seen a frogfish for over twenty years.

The list went on: I saw a rockfish, flounders, and shy red-striped squirrel fish hiding in deep holes. Next, I noticed calico eels slithering beneath me, as tiny black and white domino damselfish, no bigger than dimes, flicked back and forth over their coral head of choice. The mornings became very special to me.

Being so close to "my hike," I desperately wanted to attempt it, so I begged John to take me to the trailhead one afternoon. I had not been able to hike Wa'ahila for years. With much anticipation, we drove up the steep and curvy road to the parking lot. I got out of the car, and breathed in the familiar damp, warm pine and jungle smells that brought back so many wonderful memories to me.

As you can imagine, it was a bad idea. We perilously walked halfway up the first slippery hill, but once the trail turned into a mud bog, we were forced to turn around. It was like walking on a ski slope in Montana, rather than a Hawaiian hiking trail. We gripped onto the flexible strawberry guava branches to keep us from falling. I can't imagine it would have been good for me in a neck brace to go shooting down the lumpy, muddy, trail. To keep me from doing that, my sweet, patient, John had to hold my hand and support me all-the-way back to the car. I'm glad we tried "my hike," but the vacation was catching up to me. I was exhausted, but dad had a special occasion planned for us all, and I hoped I could make it.

THE MORNING OF OUR big outing, I woke up and I could barely get out of bed. The reservation was set up, by my dad, months ahead of our arrival and everyone was really excited to go, all except me. The thought of standing in line, then taking a shuttle bus—that was who knows how bumpy—and then standing in line some more, seemed overwhelming and too much for me to handle. Maybe they would let me nap in the late Doris Duke's Egyptian cotton sheet bed while my family enjoyed the tour—well, perhaps not.

I urged John, my dad, and sister, to head out on their own to "Shangri La." This masterpiece is the home of Doris Duke who fell in love with Middle Eastern, Asian, and Egyptian architecture, mosaics, and antiques, at a young age while traveling. She spent the next 60 years collecting and re-assembling the gorgeous artworks in her cliff-top mansion. At times, she even sat for hours by herself attaching some of the mosaic tiles she had brought home. Before her passing, she wanted to share her collection with the world, and made her home into a museum. My dad was disappointed I was not going with them, but understood, and they begrudgingly left me at home.

Propped up on blue flowered, and aloha print pillows, neck brace holding me together, my hands comfortingly felt the small ridges of the pastel-colored, well-loved, cotton quilt that was draped over me. It was so soft and thin after years of washing, and then drying on the clothesline out back under the avocado tree, where countless bathing suits hung after exhilarating days on beaches or kayaking.

Wild birds periodically rustled through fallen leaves, as mopeds sped by, and Aztec doves comfortingly cooed. The ever present trade winds occasionally filled the room, carrying the scent of plumerias and salty air, while slightly moving the leaves in a vase of long-stemmed tropical flowers, lovingly set out by my stepmom. The breeze slowly turned a driftwood and goose mobile hanging above an antique wood dresser, with slightly warped draws, that never did close right.

A text would buzz on my phone, accompanied by a smile on my face at the images from John, Joanna, and dad. They were so kind, sending me pictures as I lay in bed, so I could 'go along' on the tour with them. I grabbed my phone and looked away from the framed pictures of dogs gambling, a long-departed family member with an enormous beard and an intense look in his eyes, and my grandpa, holding the biggest salmon he had ever caught. The comedic family selfies being sent to me of their silly faces next to Doris's brightly colored mosaics and carved wooden doors was heartening.

Books, shells, feathers, barnacle-encrusted bottles, and carvings from some far-flung country filled the built-in shelves painted mint green. The leis given to us upon arrival hung on brass hooks next to an old lantern perched under a Balinese wall hanging.

I realized while slowly admiring my dad and stepmom's collections from their lives and travels around the world that I had never really stopped to look and admire everything. On past visits, I only casually glanced or quickly looked while throwing my carryon in the middle of the bed and grabbing my bathing suit, in anticipation of jumping in the ocean after being away from the islands for so long.

Another text, or three, or four, would buzz in, distracting and delighting me again between resting and glancing at an old kayak leaning against the fence outside next to a Japanese glass buoy, and a wooden pig, as fish tanks bubbled quietly in another room. I almost fell asleep, until they bounded in, the front door opened in a clatter of talking, laughter, and the re-cap of their outing.

AFTER A LOT MORE REST, days later, we drove around the island to Kailua and met up with my brother and his cute little girlfriend. They had rented a small, breezy bungalow, near the beach. We barbecued at their cottage, and then we all walked to the beach together, with flip-flops, sarongs, and boogie boards in tow.

My stepmom and I stayed on the sand in canvas beach chairs, watching them all body surf and play in the waves for a long time. Feeling a bit dejected for a *moment*, I went for a nice walk by myself along the beach, as the sun started to set, before heading back to the jovial, sandy crew. We had the best time together on that trip, getting our fill of barbeques, laughter, birthday gifts, and snorkeling. But, eventually, the merry, sun-baked group had to fly back to the mainland.

I was the only one who had planned on staying longer in Hawaii. So, when everyone else left, the task of shampooing my hair, and yanking my swimsuit up, fell to my stepmom. We both felt awkward, but it was good for a nice laugh in the mornings.

ON THE WAY HOME to Montana, I opted for an upgrade to first class, which made all the difference in the world. They even had warm chocolate chip cookies and milk for the passengers.

When I boarded the plane, the pilot teased me, saying, "You shouldn't ride those bucking broncos," so I told him it was a shark attack (in mock seriousness), and he laughed in surprise.

Strangers waiting to board smiled and told me I had a "good thing going on" for cutting in line with my neck brace, as I took my seat before the rest of the passengers. Sitting stiff and sideways in my seat, I watched the happy tourists and travelers pass by me, one by one, with newly tanned bodies, leis around their necks, aloha shirts on, and some carrying boxed pineapples. As the plane pushed back from the gate, I had time to take a deep breath and reflect.

Sometimes, I now call myself a brave chicken, but then Kelsey laughs and says, "More like just a chicken," since I tend to be a worrywart. But, erring on the side of caution and being a little paranoid, comes with the territory after going through what I had. It is very difficult, when you are deep in the dark and scary woods, not knowing if, or when, you may ever find your way out. It is such a relief when somehow, a force much greater than ourselves carries us over the threshold and back to life. Gratitude filled my heart, as I realized that even immense good could come out of terrible, or difficult, circumstances as we lifted into the air and headed over the ocean.

I pray to God that I have learned all the lessons I needed to, so I never have to go back again. I am also reminded that the only way to find home lights glowing warmly through the windows is in the midst of the some of the darkest nights.

It's silly, but back in Missoula, I found myself curled up at night, lying on my pillow, listening to John and Sunny softly breathing in the dark, and thanked God for the new life I had been given, marveling at the kindness and grace of it all. Even though I was a wimpy, whining, scaredy-cat who had complained the whole way, someone still loved me enough to guide me in the right direction: to a love and a home to share with a wonderful person, and our two fuzzy babies. I could never have imagined this course for my life, nor would I have even known how to strive for it. I don't say this to brag, or to be boastful, I am just truly grateful.

Being in bed, tucked between Sunny and my "Hunny," is like an egg, ham, and spring mix sandwich on an English muffin, dripping with butter—warm and delicious.

It was on one of those nights, after a delectable Valentine's Day dinner out at Saw-Wa-Dee Thai Restaurant, laying in bed together with the lights out, listening to a song about true companions, that John slipped an engagement ring on my finger, and asked me to marry him . . .

Heart welling, I said yes.

John and I on the North shore of Oahu.
© Dad

Families are like cookies,
they're better with a few nuts.

Mokuna 17: **Three More Months with My Last Name**

If it wasn't for pumpkins, I may not exist.

My last name first appeared in America during the 1600's. As much as I have gleaned from family stories and websites, I have a *very* rare maiden name. Only about three thousand of us have had the name, and everyone is a direct relative. It was changed when our collective, great-great-great-great—well you get the point—grandfather stepped foot off the boat, and onto Rhode Island. No one will ever know the reason why he changed his last name: hard to pronounce, fleeing persecution of some kind, or just for the heck of it (It wouldn't be totally out of line, with my family's personality). He bought a farm, built a modest stone house, married a lovely woman, and started a family.

One fall night, they were all massacred in their home—all but one boy, who was hidden in a large stove by a Native American woman. She saved him, and then carried the last remaining person on Earth with my maiden name to her village. He was traded back to his surviving maternal grandparents, in exchange for a wagon full of pumpkins. So, every fall, I buy a special pumpkin to honor that one survivor of my line. If it weren't for him, that kind woman, and pumpkins, I might not exist. For many years, we just called him the "pumpkin boy." Later, I was tracked down by a woman working on our family's genealogy, and we finally had a first name. Now I know my exact bloodline (on the men's side at least), women seem to be harder to track, unfortunately. And this is how it goes: Francis (a man), then John (the pumpkin boy), John Junior, Nathan, John, Milton, Milton Sterling, Cassius, Robert, and then my dad.

There have been pickle factories that held the name, a street in Los Angeles, land reserves, a school, and some more things I don't know about. We have been botanists, pastors, soldiers, real estate brokers, business entrepreneurs, bar and kayak store owners, teachers, artisans, master woodworkers, muralists—the list goes on, and on, and even includes a pro-kayaker from the Philippines.

Many people with my maiden name still live on Rhode Island. There is even a monument erected, in a field, honoring Francis. When the pumpkin boy grew up, he moved back to the farm, re-built the crumbling house, and raised his own family there.

After researching the battle of Gettysburg, I was shocked to find only two men with our last name listed. One fought for the South, and one fought for the North. They both died of fatal wounds on the same day. I wonder if they knew, they were fighting against their own family member on that bloody battleground. I have often wondered if they were, by some terrible chance of coincidence, responsible for each other's deaths on that fateful day.

The family always thought we were part Mohawk Indian, but that has never been proven.

My dad's dad, Robert, was the youngest of fourteen kids, by my great-grandfather's second wife. He was born in a small mountain town in Colorado. His parents died when he was barely a teenager, so he was moved to the Oregon Coast, and raised by some of his siblings. Eventually, he struck out on his own and put himself through law school. He was glad to be away from the cold, tight, deep, valley in the mountains, and living by the ocean.

WHEN I LIVED in Boulder, Colorado, my dad and stepmom flew all the way from Hawaii to visit me. We wanted to see where Grandpa had been born, and where some of the best and purest white marble in the world was quarried. On our drive up the long, twisty, mountain roads, a hail storm pounded the rental car (in August), to their shock and awe. When we arrived in the town, the amusingly pasty-looking locals gave my dad and stepmom pause. I may have even seen a brief look of fear in my dad's eyes.

First Street was labeled by a crooked wooden sign nailed to a tree, kitty-corner from one of the cutest little banks I have ever seen. The square brick building had a large room with windows in the front, a few desks, one ornate teller counter, and was completed by a large safe with gold scrollwork, free-standing against the back wall. That was it.

In one of the only gift shops in the tiny town, we were met by a lean, overall-clad, grass-chewing, local man. With the long piece of grass wiggling as he chewed, hanging from the corner of his mouth, he said, "You folks make yourself at home now; let me know if you have any questions." Of course, my curious and personable dad obliged.

As I browsed over squeaky wooden floorboards, past homemade trinkets, crafts, and postcards, looking for some memento or snack to buy, I heard the local say, "Lived here all my life, except the *war*."

He then showed my dad a dusty pair of books containing some of the history of Marble, CO. We bought the books and two white handmade marble candle holders right away. We were happily surprised to find great-grandpa listed in the books for dolling out bootlegging charges, fines, and even a ticket to a woman whose mule got loose—wreaking havoc on the unsuspecting town. There was even a brief mention of one of my grandpa's sisters being an honor student in grade school.

That night we stayed in a quaint, one-room rental cabin. The bathroom facility (an outhouse) was over a bridge, across a pond, and tucked next to the forest in some overgrown grass. Our 'room' had sheets for window coverings and a single bare bulb in the middle of the ceiling, for light. My stepmom was scared of running into strangers or being eaten by dangerous Rocky Mountain wildlife, so she refused to use the outhouse alone. Instead, to our amusement, she relieved herself behind the cabin in some trees, hidden by the dark of night.

THE NEXT DAY, we hiked up a rickety wooden boardwalk, with antique rusty nails and bolts, precariously holding it onto the mountainside, past a sign we chose to ignore which warned:

DANGEROUS

DO NOT WALK ON

Well, I am my dad's daughter, and luckily we didn't tumble screaming into the gaping maw below us, lined with jagged, gray, rocks, like monstrous, gnashing fangs.

As we reached the top of the trail leading to the quarry entrance, we noticed massive blocks of marble that had been tossed into the steep narrow creek, appearing as if they were giant discarded sugar cubes.

After our strenuous hike, we stopped for a well-earned snack. I still have a picture of a chipmunk near the path, which popped out from behind one of the gleaming chunks of marble, and was brave enough to eat out of my dad's hand.

MY DAD AND GRANDPA Robert butted heads, like many fathers and sons do. But, to me, grandpa was a silly, oddball friend, who always made me laugh. While visiting for Christmas, my dad, Uncle Jim, and grandpa, would all be in the kitchen at the same time, happily whistling and cooking up a storm. To this day, I still love it when I hear someone whistle when they cook. He called me peanut butter and, ironically, pumpkin. After dinner, he often brought a gallon of ice cream into the sunroom and slapped away any attempt by me to dive in with a spoon.

"No! You eat ice-cream with a butter knife only!" He said with a smile and a wink.

He did not like Christmas trees, so we had to hang ornaments on a 70's style, dark green, macramé masterpiece in the shape of a tree. It was hung proudly above the open, red-bricked fireplace. Instead of Christmas music, he wound up his windup toys all at once, causing a great cacophony of noise, as a monkey in a vest banged on its cymbals, wiener dogs barked, lions roared, and many others sounded off, all at once, in his living room.

Despite the festive air, there was one main person missing during those holiday visits. My dad said my grandma who passed when I was very young, from emphysema, was a kind, friendly woman, who he had been particularly close to. She raised terriers and had aspirations to be a pilot. But, woman's liberation had not quite caught up with her, before she married and began raising a family of her own. I didn't know her very well, but I always felt a strong bond between us.

Later in life, I spent weekends visiting my grandpa and his new wife in Issaquah. She decorated their house "to the teeth" with blue country florals, vibrant clown paintings, swan décor, and vintage train memorabilia. Her father had worked as a train engineer for much of his life. The only time I ever saw her jump up and down and scream, "Wooo wooo!" is when she and grandpa dropped me off at a train station and the locomotive arrived. She also loved grandfather clocks and dolls, so *of course* we had to mischievously sneak one of his small snapping metal alligators onto one of her treasured baby doll's hair. Then we stuck it on top of one of her many clocks and waited in anticipation for the inevitable, "Robert!" We tried to hide, but let out large, belly-rolling, laughs together while ducking behind the couch, out of her line of sight.

She would get us back.

We were sitting on the deck, enjoying the sunshine and watching golfers. All of a sudden she snuck up behind us, and, right as they were about to swing, she blew her antique hunting horn. Then she scampered back into the house laughing, letting us get the dirty looks and angry comments from the golfers.

But, if she thought she had won that round, my grandpa had a surprise in store for her. She refused to let him have a cat. So, he bought a fake white cat, with motion activated purring, and, delighted with himself, sat in front of her as her eyes rolled, petting it triumphantly with a big grin and a wink.

She was a tough lady though, full of piss and vinegar, but she was not brave enough to walk my grandpa's dog. His name was Pookey, and he was a small, white, fluffy, dog. I took him out any chance I had because when he went to take a pee, he walked on his front paws and a bright yellow stream of urine arched through the air. I never grew tired of walking him. My grandpa once had an offer from a Circus owner to buy Pookey, but he could never part with his little, funny, friend.

AFTER VISITING COLORADO, I asked my mom's dad, Bill, about his life and parents. One of my favorite pictures is of his dad as a young man, sitting astride his horse. His father and a couple of his siblings are outside of their rustic split log house, and in the lower right corner is a black and white dog wearing a frilly bonnet. I guess girls will be girls in any age, and dogs will continue to wear our bonnets.

He loved to tell me the story of a little neighbor girl who picked his mother's flowers, came to the door as proud as could be, and gave them to her as a gift. His mother just graciously smiled and thanked the little girl, never having the heart to scold her.

When he was a young boy, his dad Allan left him alone in their Model-T Ford truck, idling on the streets of Seattle, while he ran an errand. Out of nowhere a fire truck raced by. With his legs barely long enough to reach the pedals, he stretched up on tippy toes, his nose just clearing the steering wheel, and took off down the street after them, determined to see the fire. He said the scolding that followed was worth it. Just out of high school, he sold fresh fish out of the back of that same Ford before he went to college.

It was during college, before his business bloomed, that he met my grandma Pearl, who was in nursing school. They were soon engaged, and stayed married for more than fifty years. She had been raised on a farm in the wind-swept flatlands of North Dakota. She said they ate almost every part of the animals they raised and butchered, and she took baths in small metal tubs in the middle of the kitchen, while her mom continued to pour hot water in it from the wood stove.

After being raised mainly in the grasslands, she wouldn't allow my grandpa to cut down any unnecessary trees when they built their houses together on Bainbridge Island. She was in awe of them, thinking they were so special after growing up without them. When she died, her ashes were spread in a circle around a grand old cedar tree.

THINKING ABOUT THE PAST, contemplating the future, newly engaged, and turning forty years old, my dad called to wish me a Happy Birthday. In his backwards, hilarious, joking way he said, "Congratulations, you're half dead." Had I finished half of a life, or was I just starting a new one?

I couldn't have made it through without my family, friends, angels, and the love of my loyal dog. I am grateful to them, and to the memories of Manitou beach, tide flats, hikes in jungle forests, ferry boats, sand between my toes, jellyfish, trees and all they give and sacrifice for us, robins singing, crow caws hanging in the cool spring air, healing nature spirits, baby fish, my horse, warm apple pies in the fall, perfect snowflakes, sand dollars, and more than I could ever remember or list. These things carried me, nurtured me, and kept me warm and safe, in my darkest hours. I am so thankful for the grace I received, for the lessons of the past, the promise of my future right around the corner, and a wedding to a good-hearted man. Without the trauma and extreme life change that I endured, I would never have lived in Montana with my best friend, become bonded to my brother and sister again, or met my wonderful John.

The day was coming fast, soon we would be married.

Great-grandpa Allan astride his horse on the homestead in Nebraska next to his father, siblings, and the dog wearing a bonnet.

© Great-grandma ?

Grandma Pearl Madonna as a girl. Her mother took the picture and she wrote this poem.

"This little girl is five years old. Was born and raised in weather hot and cold near Logan, North Dakota. Her mom loved to take photos, and while we were nestled in bed at night, she developed them just right. Even in homemade woolen knickers, that probably brought many snickers, this one she did of one little kid. Guess who?"

1925 on the farm

© Great-grandma (mom's side)

The family built it.
It hides within the mountains,
no cell phone service.

The family's cabin.
© C.M. Arvish

Mokuna 18: **I Do**

I had these lines prepared about how this was the first day I would walk into my new life, the first sunrise and first sunset . . . Yeah, well that's nice and all, but this is what really happened: the good, the bad, and the psychotic breakdown of it all.

Our wedding was to be held at my fiancé's great-grandfather's cabin. It was built on a creek above Yellowstone as both a family cabin and a way station for himself and his wife, since he was the first county health officer in the area. They gathered rocks from all over the canyon and hand built a beautiful multi-colored fireplace and chimney. As the family grew, so did a screened-in sleeping porch. There have been many family reunions, getaways, weddings, and generations who have loved this simple primitive place.

The cabin is set at the base of a mossy green canyon, with climbing rocks and hiking trails leading out the back door, and framed with the sounds of a small creek, happily bubbling past.

There is a "log book" made with a real split log and sheets of brown paper bags chronicling peoples' visits, and messages starting back in the 30's. I loved the cute little notes next to peace signs from a small boy, who is now the man I was going to marry, about enjoying his visits there.

We found an old note from a man in the 70's, who was hitchhiking his way up the highway from California and was caught in a terrible snow storm. In desperation, he found the cabin and sheltered there for the night. He left money for the coffee he drank, and a message of thanks. In a post script he left a prediction for 1974 as well, that Nixon would be impeached.

WE ARRIVED A COUPLE of days before everyone else to clean and spiff up the place, make all the beds with mismatched thrift store sheets, and add little gifts on pillows of natural essential oil infused perfumes, and chocolates. The plan was to have some of our closest friends and family members arrive early and camp out with us, enjoying this slice of rustic Montana living. We loved to tease the out-of-towners with stories of the outhouse, bears, and the reality of no cell phone service.

John filled the large water jugs that sit next to the sink for dishes since there is no running water. There *is* power now, but I love the cabin at night with the lights off, just some candles and the fireplace glowing. A couple of couches, a dining room table, and some chairs filled the rest of the rustic space. My mom stayed in the "suite," the only bedroom not on the screened-in sleeping porch. It had an antique wooden dresser with an attached vanity mirror full of time-worn charm, a small bed, and a curtain for a door. *That* was fancy.

In reality, we were visiting the mice's house. They climbed over the rocks around the fireplace, along wooden edges, and even fell into the sink at times. We expected that Sunny was going to chase them like squirrels, but to our surprise, he went, tail wagging, up to this tiny mouse in the middle of the living room floor and touched noses with it, as we laughed in disbelief.

My mom, to her surprise, had a "tiny fluffy creature" visit her in the night; falling right on her head. She said she didn't scream, she just calmly checked the blankets to make sure it wasn't in bed with her, and went back to sleep.

John and my mom are early birds. So, in the mornings, as Sunny and I stayed nice and warm under the covers, they made aromatic French press coffee and started a crackling fire in the large wood stove. John loved to read by the bubbling creek in the early morning light, with a delicious steaming cup in his hand, while birds sang in the trees around him.

During the warmest part of the day, the creek had pools just big enough to float in and have a rustic bath. I love this wonderful place, and we were very privileged to be able to be married there.

At a previous family reunion, I met John's great aunt Constance, who is the last person alive that witnessed the building of the cabin.

Holding both of my hands in hers she said, "*Guess* what age I am."

She looked to be eighty at the most, so I guessed that.

Then, she drew numbers in the air with a coy smile, whispering loudly, "*One*, zero, zero."

I couldn't believe it! She was bending over better than I was, joking with everyone, and insisting she always needed her eggs and bacon for breakfast.

She told us about coming to the canyon with her parents, and camping at Ousel Falls when she was a little girl, before the cabin had been built. When we asked her permission to have our wedding there, excitedly she said, "Of course, I love weddings at the cabin!"

With a few days to go, my mom and I quickly set out to find the perfect spot for the living arbor, and we found it between two small pine trees perfectly set on the edge of the creek. After gathering and binding curved branches to the trees with jute string, we were happy with our first day of building. Later, my brother's brand new wife did a beautiful job fleshing out the arch with greens, flowers, gauzy material, and a bird's nest that John had spotted on the dirt road. The small creation of curved twigs and soft fluff was perfect since we had birdhouses, nests, and little pairs of birds as part of the decorations.

My dad, stepmom, and sister relished the drive from the airport to the cabin; enjoying the new sights, sounds, and spotting wildlife as we followed the twisting river down the canyon. Twenty minutes before reaching our destination, we stopped in Big Sky for ice cream and were met with allegations of exaggerating the remoteness of the cabin.

"But it was so fun to hear you squirm," we admitted.

My dad has visited cannibals in the dark jungles of New Guinea, but he is scared of a Montana two-holer? "Big pantie!" I said, throwing one of his favorite sayings back at him. We had to rub that one in. But, like the good daughter that I am, I cleaned a toilet seat, painted his name on the lid, and hung it lovingly from a nail in the outhouse, primed for his arrival. Later he said he appreciated it, but without fasteners, the seat slid around on him when he used it, which made it all the funnier to me.

In the meantime, Kelsey and Fred arrived in their camper van, parking it out back. No sooner had Kelsey stepped out of the van door than we were up the hiking trail, scouting out wildflowers for my bouquet. Amazingly, my sister, the tech-head, was brave enough to come with us, once I explained that the trail was well maintained and used all year around. I still laugh when I think of her flapping her hands, slightly annoyed, saying, "The nature is touching me!" when small leaves and branches brushed her legs as we made our way up the valley.

Back at the cabin, we talked and laughed as we hung the homemade pennants that I had attached to long jute twine. They scalloped along the front of the proud-looking cabin and in-between trees, framing our arbor as they flicked and danced in the breezy sunshine.

One mom was making large paper flowers in the homey shade of the cabin, while the other one was setting up the areas for our Luau and Yum tables.

A delicious local bakery and pottery shop was slated to have the spice cake, slathered with maple frosting, as well as a multitude of goodies fresh and ready for pick-up on the morning of the wedding. I realized, while watching my two moms busy as bees with wedding preparations, that I would have four moms when John and I were married.

Well, four are better than one, I jested to myself.

SOME OF US decided to head to Yellowstone National Park for a day trip. I had only seen pictures and heard stories, never having been there myself yet. It truly did not disappoint. With every turn of the road, we saw elk, bison, antelope, ravens, and red dragonflies buzzing around hot steaming spouts of boiling crystal blue water. The scenery changed so quickly, and the sites were so intriguing, I almost ran out of things to say—*almost.*

We stopped by Old Faithful Inn, a large log hotel, custom-built with not a square corner in sight. Gorgeous gnarly wood twisted around door frames and up the railings on all levels. I tried to climb to the cupola, but it had been closed due to safety concerns after a large earthquake from the late 50's had left it in less than stable condition.

We watched the Old Faithful geyser spout high into the air, while seated in log chairs on the main veranda, among a chorus of exuberant tourists. Afterwards, down in the main lobby, I snapped a picture of my dad and stepmom goofing off, as they pretended to be eaten by an enormous carved grizzly bear statue.

WELL, AS FAMILIES ALWAYS do, we had some members that we were concerned about how they might behave at the wedding—one in particular, who has a flair for the dramatics. My fiancé's cousin Sandy could be unpredictable at the best of times, so we were worried about her arrival.

The other cousin Gina, who was arriving with Sandy, is great: funny, spunky, strong, in your face, and brave enough to get into Ousel Falls with me and crawl under the sheet of freezing water, while we laughed and smiled at each other. She took it upon herself to have a "talking to" with Sandy, laying down the law. She could not get drunk, or have alcohol anywhere around the cabin or at the wedding. She promised to behave, but the memory of her hi-jinks and off-colored jokes at a previous family outing kept playing in my head. So, Gina was nice enough to bring her along, but they were planning on pitching tents a couple of miles away and *not* staying at the cabin. Sure enough, when they arrived, it was raining cats and dogs!

"Stay the night in the cabin, and pitch tents tomorrow," we said, wanting to be welcoming.

Most of the day went well, but just before bed Sandy started to vigorously make herself comfortable in the upper bunk of a flimsy teenagers' metal bunk-bed, above my sister's head. All that was holding it together were small screws, bolts, and a wish and a prayer. I saw my sister's eyes widen as she noticed the shimmy, shake, groan and strain of the bunk bed. She politely excused herself, saying that she was much more comfortable on the couch in the living room due her hip hurting. Joanna delicately ran away in fear of being squashed in the middle of the night, and it's a good thing that she did.

It started slowly, as all occurrences do in cabins way back in the woods, while everyone is asleep in the dark with no cell phone service. At first, the conversations, we thought, must have been between Gina's daughter Rebecca and herself. They must not be able to sleep, we discussed under the covers, giving her the benefit of the doubt.

Then came the running hurriedly around the cabin in the dark, slamming doors, while exclaiming, "I can't find my coat! I can't find my book!" Then, she was rummaging in the bushes, talking to unseen people about how she lost her flashlight. Now, using her lighter—in an old flammable cabin—to find other items she had misplaced, her speech pattern eerily changed into a gravelly, sinister, man's voice to answer herself during conversations.

I thought she was possessed.

She slammed more doors and tried to talk to my stepmom who peeked over the blankets she had pulled over her nose and mouth, nervously curled up under her covers in bed.

I cringed and slightly giggled every time my dad got up to use the outhouse since she followed him outside in the dark while asking strange questions.

My dad and stepmom ran Anna Bannana's, their bar, for years, and had experience with eclectic characters, so I thought they could handle this, and it's a good thing that my family has a great sense of humor.

John put Sandy back to bed several times.

Up she bolted, running around again and again. She started telling him that all the voices were talking to her, telling her what to do. She was teaching them to make things with sticks and rocks, and they were teaching her things too, and she hated what the voices were saying, and she was praying and talking to them trying to get them to go away.

As the night deepened, she started hovering over our bed, standing there in the dark as I held close to John, and latched onto Sunny's dog collar, to keep him from going towards her.

She stood still, and stared ominously down at us, saying, "Young people get to flip, why can't I?" Then, a mad rant about an apartment she rented.

I almost expected to see a knife in her hand, rearing up and glinting in the moonlight above our heads.

My stepmom, while laughing, later confessed she was thinking "*Oh great*, the classic deep-in-the woods cabin massacre!"

When Sandy finally told John that she kept waking up standing on the edge of the highway not knowing how she got there, *that* was it. To keep her safe, John woke up Gina to help and ushered her outta there.

They gathered her up, to sobs and wails of, "You are *taking* me from my *cousin's wedding!*"

He responded, "It is not safe, you cannot stay here!"

At three o'clock in the morning, Gina and Rebecca took Sandy to a hospital, while she blamed Gina and tried to jump out of the moving vehicle several times.

We were all adrenalized and awake, laughing and telling each other of our versions of the happenings, with lots of oh mys, holy cows, and *geez*.

My sista (sees-ta), as I call her, started coffee, and said she was happy she made up an excuse early-on not to sleep under Sandy's bed.

When the sun came up, we found, next to the creek, the almost empty Snapple bottle with wine still in it. When Gina came back to the cabin, we found out Sandy had accidentally taken multiple sleeping pills with the wine. She said she kept forgetting that she had taken one, so she took another and another, until she started hallucinating and became delusional.

After running into Big Sky for supplies, John received many texts from Sandy, apologizing and begging to come back. We had a long discussion, and decided that we were not comfortable allowing her back, so, we gingerly asked her not to return. This wasn't about her, but about focusing on our fun and lovely wedding.

I couldn't wait to fill in my brother and his new wife regarding our crazy night when they arrived the next day, after rumbling up the dirt road in their car. I knew they would understand.

Even at their wonderful wedding in Whistler, Canada, the month before—where we all had a fabulous time—one of his friends got drunk and was arrested by Canadian Mounties within six hours of crossing the border. A new record for him, we were told. I love the story as my brother tells it. His friend wasn't pissed about being arrested, handcuffed, and being laid face down on the cement street, but about the Mounties describing him as a "portly" gentleman when they called it in. He said angrily to the police, "*Who* are you calling *portly*?!"

So, my brother had the arrest, and we had the "psychotic episode."

We put the crazy day, or night I should say, behind us and enjoyed readying the cabin for the festivities.

Wildflower bouquet,
the forest all around us,
white lace and side arms.

The wonderful Ousel Falls.
© *C.M. Arvish*

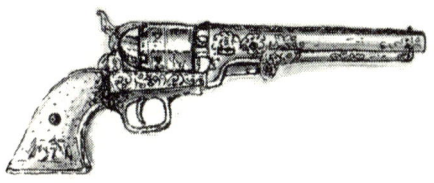

Mokuna 19: **I Do Too**

The plan was for my sister Joanna and Kelsey to stay with me in a fancy log hotel a few miles up the road the night before, and then help me get dressed in the morning.

My sister was appalled at the idea of Kelsey and me hiking to the falls the morning of the ceremony. "Great! All we need is for you guys to get lost, or be eaten by a bear, before your wedding!"

John reassuringly backed us up, saying, "*Ah*, these two? *They'll be fine.*"

So, on we went.

Up at the crack of dawn we headed out, in colorful leggings, tennis shoes, and bathing suits. I had been to Ousel Falls the previous day with a group of family and friends, and we agreed it rivaled some of the prettiest falls we had ever seen—even in Hawaii. The falls had two of my favorite aspects. The first was a rock "bench" to sit on, where the water falls all around your shoulders. Or if you wanted to brave the cold, one could duck behind the pounding curtain of water to get a real thrill. It also had a deeper pool under a cave-like rock ledge, perfect for floating in, as any self-respecting water nymph would. I was very excited to show Kelsey. We had a great time and *weren't* even eaten by bears.

Arriving back, safe and sound, the butterflies were already starting to do cartwheels in my belly as I stepped into a warm shower.

They primped and preened, and curled and quaffed. Then, makeup was added, and something was padded, as they laced me into my sweet summer dress. It was long in the back and short in the front, with thin white layers hanging like petals. A short sleeved lace bolero jacket covered my shoulders and flat shoes with tiny white flowers on my feet. A birdcage veil was placed on my head, adorned with white feathers and pearls. A handmade necklace with old buttons and shells was hung around my neck. My lips were the last to be added, bright red as a bunch of cherries. When I looked in the mirror, I saw looking back the bright, breezy, vintage bride I had hoped for. They spirited me away, careful as the secret service, and down the road we went, headed to our final destination.

I was snuck into the cabin while John hid in the woodshed, my tears kept at bay with prayers from our cute-as-a-button officiate (a woman even tinier than Kelsey if you can believe that), and my new sister-in-law, smacking me on my butt with a fan every few minutes to distract me. I waited nervously as the guests arrived and took their seats.

I peeked through the curtains and saw the faces of my friends and family waiting for me to appear.

Sunny was decked out in his hula skirt and lei ring-bearer outfit. He was the first to exit the cabin, while everyone laughed and smiled, led by Kelsey, her long flower skirt flowing next to him.

The day before had been windy and rainy, but this morning the weather had softened into a perfectly warm sunny day with gentle breezes.

As I stood waiting to leave the cabin, a wave of gratitude washed over me for how far I had come and amazed at being transported into a life and place I had never even imagined being, and was so much better for it.

The time had come.

"First Gymnopedie," by Erik Satie, played as we stepped out the door; tears in my eyes and the wild-flower bouquet gripped in my trembling hand. The soft wind lifted up my skirt as we left the cabin and entered the sunlight. My dad held my arm, leading me along the rock-lined outdoor aisle, in his aloha shirt and shorts. I was nervous to speak in front of everyone and share my innermost feelings of love with my almost-husband, so I focused only on John, in his linen pants, light blue cool cotton shirt, and aloha vest covered in orchids. Tears rolled down his cheeks as we approached him, and he delicately took hold of my hands.

The surprised look on John's face was precious when his adopted Native American brother and girlfriend appeared carrying an eagle feather, sage, and an abalone shell as they smudged us before the ceremony started.

After an opening prayer, a poem was read as we simultaneously poured sand from Hawaii, Washington State, and Montana into a square glass jar, ceremoniously blending our lives and loves together. All in attendance were asked to write their names on shells and rocks piled in small silver bowls after the ceremony, and add it to the jar.

Our surroundings became quiet, as an expectant hush fell on the gathering. Even the breeze and birds, as if in anticipation, were silent.

John spoke first.

"Sweetie, from the first time we met, I knew there was something different, something special about you. You have a light in you that touches everything you do. Friend, partner, painter, lover, singer of silly songs, lover of animals and of nature. You have a sense of freedom, joy, and adventure that fills my heart. I never dreamed it could be possible to find a partner like that. One who accepts and loves me, with all my passions in life, as well as my foibles and faults. One who accepts all of me, unconditionally. I am so happy with our life and so proud to call you mine and to affirm that today with the people we love. I love you."

I didn't know if I could speak after that, but I just focused on his pretty eyes, took a breath, and spoke just to him.

"Hunny; I am happy to stand here today, and tell you that I love you. You came into my life in a very unexpected way by the grace of God, and I am thankful every day. You are a light in my life, and I thank you for your kindness, your sweet heart, and your loving arms that you wrap around me. I am happy to share our home and our lives together along with our babies. I am grateful for us, and I am happy to become your wife today. I love you, aloha nui loa."

We exchanged I dos and rings; my white gold band, inlaid with multi-colored sapphires from Montana, sparkled in the sunlight.

"You may now kiss the groom," the officiate said, in a pre-planned joke.

We kissed for the first time as man and wife to cheers and the ringing of a wind chime as we stood under the arbor, with gauzy fabric blowing in the air around us.

We ran around the woods having pictures taken of ourselves next to trees and rocks, on top of a small footbridge, and in bare feet, kicking up water as we braced each other in the refreshing creek.

The day was wonderful, and we were about to start eating when the *sheriff* arrived. Two of the most important people had not shown up, and now we knew why.

John's mom had not been feeling well and said she was not sure she could make it, but wanted us to go on with our special day. She went to the hospital that morning to be "patched up," and then headed towards the cabin. They came within six miles when she had an allergic reaction to a medication and went into anaphylactic shock, having to be transported by emergency personnel out of the canyon. They almost lost her, but she was resuscitated on the way to the hospital.

We raced up the highway until we found a cell phone signal, and called his stepfather immediately. His weary and rattled voice emanated from the speakerphone as he started to relay what had happened to John's mom. He said, "While they waited for the emergency vehicle he had begged her not to leave him as she lay near death in the back of their camper van." He didn't want to go into details but said, "She is stabilized now and will be kept in intensive care at least overnight and maybe for a few days." "We are on our way," we said.

As we drove towards the hospital, they were adamant that she was okay and a little embarrassed, and did not want us or anyone to leave the wedding to go to her. So, we passed on our message of love, and said we were happy that she was safe. Satisfied that she was in good hands, we headed back to the cabin.

Luckily, everyone had been enjoying the Kalua Pork with Hawaiian sea salt, poi, rice, and salad on the luau table while we were gone. Our guests were happy John's mom was fine, and in the late afternoon, after their fill of spice cake, started to trickle away from the festivities, congratulating and hugging us as they went.

After most of the party had gone, we headed back to Buck's T-4, the beautiful rustic and elegant, split-log and stone lodge. We settled in and ate expertly cooked gourmet meals of Mahi Mahi (a menu special) and a delectable Red Deer with wild berry sauce. Our bellies were full and satisfied with this ending of a *mostly* wonderful day.

Since some of our close friends and family were still around, we all had fun hanging out in the outdoor pools and hot tubs after dinner, until the thunder and lightning scared away even the bravest of soakers. Then, we headed to our room, to turn in for the night as man and wife. We spent the night in the comfy hotel bed, and then with the first morning light prepared to head out on our . . .

"Honeymoons."

I *WONDER* IF I am the first person in the world to say that I went on my honeymoon with my sister, stepmom, and dad, to Cody, Wyoming.

My new husband John graciously agreed I should spend more time with my family since I hadn't seen them for over a year, and we would go on a more official honeymoon later. For now, he would head home to prepare for the next school year and leave us to go touring. We helped lock up the cabin, packed our gear in the rental SUV and headed out of town.

We took our time driving through Yellowstone and past beautiful rock formations on our way to Wyoming. Once there, we stopped for dinner in Wild Bill Cody's, lovely, old-fashioned, wood, rock, and sandstone, Irma hotel. There were classic animal mounts from the region and an ornately carved wooden bar with a highly polished, beveled, mirror near our table, which reflected our smiles as we ate the best buffalo ribs we had collectively tried before.

After we were happy and full, we wanted to tour the hotel, but not Joanna. I still tease my sister, because she wouldn't come upstairs with us to see the high ceilinged, gorgeous, vintage hotel rooms filled with marble-clad dressers, antique bed-frames, and time-tested charm. She insisted the hotel was *haunted.*

As she waited for us outside, she admired the next door gunsmith's shop, which displayed, on its roof, the biggest gun she had ever seen, spanning a large corner of the building. She proudly sent pictures to her gun enthusiast boyfriend.

The next day, we visited a fantastic museum in town (The Buffalo Bill Center of the West). To our surprise, the building was expansive and offered many wonderful exhibits. Large rooms held re-creations of life-sized dwellings of both First Nations people and early settlers to the area.

Wild Bill had an entire wing to himself. Actual costumes, posters, and his traveling furniture encircled a mock theater, where old black and white footage, of his famous traveling show, continuously looped.

Downstairs, my stepmom and I found guns, guns, and more guns near an array of stuffed trophy animals. It was impressive, but not quite our thing.

Modernistic and landscape paintings hung in hallways near a fascinating installation. The museum had dismantled the living room/art studio of a dearly departed famous artist from Wyoming. Then they painstakingly re-assembled it, complete with a wax statue of the artist painting at his easel; one of his actual half-finished paintings rested under his permanently poised brush.

Next, we went to a delightfully spooky old western town, re-built just off of the highway by an archaeologist, for our historical enjoyment. Small old split-log houses, barns, carriages, and real human remains filled the grounds. Once *again*, you *guessed it*, my sister stayed in the car, *away* from the ghosts.

Our motel's pool sat in the middle of a parking lot, surrounded by a chain link fence, and covered with sand, and dust. My intrepid, water-loving, dad jumped in right away. My sister and I came ready with swimsuits and good intentions.

After our obvious hesitation, he asked, "Why you two not coming in?"

To which I replied; "Well, we have hoo haaas, so I am not about to go in *that* water."

We found out later the pool water was clean; it was just murky from the dust that blew along the range, with the tumbling tumbleweeds.

THE NEXT EVENING, we drove off, exuberantly, to the rodeo with tickets in hand. Well, when in Rome . . . (or in Cody as it were).

We partook in a great American tradition of whooping, hollering, and cheering on the rodeo riders, until my dad said, "I didn't know rodeos were so *stinky*," in his smirky, laughing way; extra buttery popcorn tumbling down from his hand into his giggling lap.

We were right above the bull and horse pens (hence the delightful aroma). But, we had the best seats in the house, right behind the release gates for the bucking broncos and bull riders.

We all agreed none of this was on any of our bucket lists, but we sure had a wonderful time in Cody, Wyoming and I have the sticker on my car to prove it.

My new husband had gone on his way/honeymoon with his buddy Dale and Sunny. They decided not to drive home with the "just married" sign on the car, no offense to anyone.

He happily said, "We *did* stop at the Dairy Queen on the way home though, living it up!"

MY MOM HAD KEPT the news from me that her dad Bill, my last remaining grandparent, had almost passed away during the wedding. I had just started a new chapter of my life and was going to make sure to be there for him in his last. Now my strong, independent, and fun grandpa needed me to hold his hand and to be the strong and brave one for him as he faced the inevitable change we all have to experience. I was home just a day and a half, with wedding money in hand, so I grabbed a flight back to Washington, to see my grandpa one last time, before he left this world.

Grandparents are only in our lives for a short time,
but they stay in our hearts forever.

*Joanna snapped one of our favorite wedding creek
pictures.*

© *Joanna*

Mokuna 20: **Grandpas; Almost Near the End**

I arrived hours later, using our wedding as an excuse. "I just had to come back, to show you our wedding pictures," I told my grandpa. I am sure he knew why but was just too nice not to be pleasant and happy that I was visiting. He smiled, enjoying the pictures from our special day, glad that he could see them.

His body had been so faithful, for almost ninety-nine years, but soon it was not going to be able to house his spirit any longer, and he would have to pass on. I sat with him many times during the day as he dozed in and out. Occasionally, he woke up and wanted to do his banking, or pack the car and head off to see his girlfriend. She had been calling him, wondering if he was coming to visit her this weekend, not fully understanding how close he was to leaving. They had both been widowed years before, becoming each other's travel, opera, and weekend companions. We assured him all the important banking and chores had been taken care of and had the phone nearby so they could speak to each other, even if briefly.

Although he was in a weakened state, he was just as easy going as always. Grandpa replied to most inquiries with, "*Sure*, why not, go *ahead*," a saying I am very fond of. Even as some of his final words in those last days were spoken, I still heard him say, "*Sure*, why not, go *ahead*." He was so friendly.

I was happy I could be there for him, and sat next to his easy chair, holding his hand which was not strong anymore, but soft, and gentle. I took in all the sights, smells, and little details around me, realizing how very fortunate I was to be raised near my grandparents; spending time with them, learning from them, and growing up on this wonderful island. The house had been the same for years and years, but now that would all be changing.

John, my sister Joanna, and I had all visited the month before on our way up to my brother Tatum's wedding in Canada. Grandpa was still chipper and making pancakes in the mornings, a delicious tradition we loved. He was so excited about the moonrise coming over the trees across the water, so we all gathered on his porch and waited each night in anticipation. Across the bay, the large bright white sphere ever-so-slowly peeked through the trees to our "ooos, awes," and accolades, then came up in all its glory, sending shimmers of light dancing across the black water. It sure was worth the wait, and he was very happy we could be there to see the moonrise with him.

He spoke of being grateful for such a wonderful family, a good life, and a beautiful place to live, telling my sister that he had, "one final great adventure left."

He and John hit it off right away, engaging in long conversations. I even heard my grandpa say what a nice fellow John was to someone on the phone.

This was the first time John had been to Bainbridge Island, so we toured around and spent time beach-combing and walking in the clear water. We put chilly, caramel-colored, kelp seaweed on my shoulders like a scarf, while admiring the myriad of colorful beach crabs hiding under sea anemone-dappled rocks. We had a delightful time, and I was happy that Grandpa was healthy right up to the very end.

As he sat, wrapped up in a warm blanket one morning on his deck, looking out onto the Puget Sound, he asked me quietly for coffee. I quickly made him a hot steaming cup and brought it to him. Independent to the last, he took the heavy cup in his trembling hands, and ever so slowly brought the cup up to his lips and took a sip, then all of a sudden he threw his head back, saying "*Ah!* There is nothing like morning coffee." I thought it was so cute.

One of my most precious moments with him came while I sat next to his overstuffed chair when he slept.

Well, I thought he was asleep, but I heard him say, "Blackberry pie . . . on the table?"

I quickly stood up and told my mom what he had said.

"Oh yes! That is one of his favorites," she said smiling, "you should go pick some for him right away, and we will make a pie."

I grabbed a small colander, briskly headed up the driveway and down the road, where I had foraged so many times before as a girl. The street past his house is narrow and lush with no sidewalks but has ample blackberry vines crawling up people's driveways and along the edges. I quickly recalled the blackberry-picking yoga, jujitsu moves I had mastered as a child, as I reached and twisted into the vines on my tiptoes, carefully avoiding the thorns. We were more than pleased to make the pie for Grandpa, and he responded with rewarding compliments.

ON ONE WARM-ISH AFTERNOON, the Puget Sound was calling me, so I headed across the yard and over the driftwood, inching my way slowly, trying not to cut my feet on the barnacles. With joyful anticipation, I entered the chilly water. It was so clear I could see all the way to the bottom. After my legs and belly were partially numb and used to the cold water, I took the plunge, dipping all the way up to my chin while hooting between quick breaths. Once submerged, I can swim pretty comfortably for a while, enjoying the top six inches of slightly warmer water. I love swimming in the Puget Sound, but when my grandpa's "sweet-as-peaches" neighbor woman called out to me from her yard, behind long beach grasses, and invited me to swim in her outdoor heated pool, I happily accepted.

We swam and floated, engaging in light-hearted chit-chat; but inevitably the conversation veered to my grandpa. She was sad to hear he might be leaving soon, and reminisced about their Orca spotting conversations together, and exclaimed, "What a nice man he is." Joanna, noticing where I was, quickly headed our way. "Sweet-as-peaches" invited us to stay the night in her guest house as my sister entered the pool. I usually do not want to intrude, but with many family members crowding the house, and childhood beds no longer feeling comfortable, we happily accepted.

That evening, after saying goodnight to Grandpa, we lugged our travel bags next door and settled in. My sister happily indulged in the wine and chocolate, left for us in the kitchenette.

"Be careful, or you will end up in one of my novels," was the sign that hung on the wall.

We smiled and laughed it off, joking that there might be a hidden camera, so we better be on our best behavior, then we quickly forgot about the warning.

I had my eye on the bathtub, adorned with fragrant bath salts and fresh soft towels, so I left my sister to her own devices and headed into the bathroom.

The water was warm as I sank into the filling tub, turning knobs with my feet to adjust the flow and temperature. I was just thinking about writing a thank you note in the guestbook when I reached up lazily through the steam to turn off the water, and to my shock, I couldn't. I turned the knobs to the left, then to the right; I tried the center knob, but it *broke* off in my hands! Water was flowing full blast and filling the tub faster than it was draining. I jumped out; half toweled and grabbed my sister for help. We couldn't shut the water off, so she Skyped her boyfriend, who was at a dinner party, on her Smartphone. In the meantime, I called John, and had him on one ear and my brother on the other, with my mom's cell phone. A neighbor up the hill was at the ready to come over and shut off the main water supply if needed. The owners were not home, so we continued to troubleshoot with our remote male counterparts.

We were almost to the point of shutting off the main valve, when my sister yelled over the fence to me that she had stopped the water. I had been with my mom as she was calling the neighbor for help. When I got back, my sister had an odd smile on her face.

"Come here," she said, amused.

She reached up, and just, yup, turned it off while laughing.

She said the magic question had come from her boyfriend, while friends surrounded him at their dinner party. He asked, "Did *you* try turning it off?"

We were laughing so hard at our ridiculousness, so I ran up to the kitchen sink, turned it on, then feigned alarm, saying, "*Help* me, *help* me sister, I *can't* turn it off!"

Had we been caught on some sort of hidden camera we wondered as I ran around half-naked, while she tried to help me, and we couldn't figure out the shower like big dorks.

Thank God the owner wasn't home; I would have been so embarrassed.

When I turned both knobs all the way to the left, the water for the shower turned off and came on for the bath. Then, when I turned the knobs all the way to the right, the opposite happened. The center knob with all the numbers appeared to be for percentages of heat and water flow. If you don't understand how I am describing the shower, that's okay, neither do I, but I thought I would try.

After all was safe, I said to my sister, "Ok, I will go back and take a shower now."

"Don't you dare!" she yelled from across the room.

After drawing a picture of a bathtub, I added a very vague explanation, in the guest book with my thanks.

I guess those newfangled showers are too complex for me; I should go back to washing in the creeks of Montana or the waterfalls of Hawaii. *They* need *no* introduction.

I couldn't wait to call Kelsey and tell her what I had done.

She laughed so hard saying, "I didn't even need to be there to play a joke on you; the universe did it for me!"

Or, I did it to myself, one of the two.

I HAD STAYED as long as I could. Knowing this was the last time I would see grandpa alive, I held his hand, bent over and kissed his cheek, and bravely smiled. Memories rolled by of walks on the beach, bon-fires, and years of his kindness. My only regret was living so far away and not visiting more. My grandma had passed on so early that I didn't have the adult realization yet regarding how precious they were. I was truly blessed to have them. *"He was a treasure,"* I thought to myself, as I told him I loved him, slowly turned, and walked away for the last time. Then, I was driven to my waiting ferry boat.

After I boarded, I sat on a white bench in the warm sun, admiring my new wedding ring. A soft breeze swirled up from the water, as the gentle vibrations increased from the large engines pushing us forward.

I watched a couple leaning over the railing on their crossed arms, chins up to the wind looking out towards Seattle, as a black and white Boston Terrier casually licked the woman's leg; she seemed not to notice or care as they watched the scenery go by. Seagulls, seaplanes, paragliders, and jellyfish swirled and flew by on their own trajectories.

I did not know when I might be here again; but my belly distracted me from my sorrow, in anticipation of the clam chowder and chips waiting for me on Pier 54 in Seattle. I deeply inhaled the salty sea air, thinking of my new husband waiting for me in Montana; and of the coming fall and snowy winter in the mountains. Another seagull effortlessly floated by, giving me a quick glance as I stared out across the waves.

I was lost in thought, thinking of ferry boat passengers as souls, arriving and departing this Earth in a never-ending loop of life and death, when the Ferry boat horn blasted, startling me back into the present. So, I rose from my bench and headed off to the next adventure.

In the beginning, I thought I was writing a story of a tragedy, but it turned out to be a story about gratitude, hope, and joy. I am amazed that my life, shaken down to its bedrock, and left in tatters, could be, by the grace of God, rebuilt into a better and more sincere life for me. And for *that*, I will be ever thankful.

THAT FOLLOWING CHRISTMAS, John was sorting and moving boxes from our bedroom, when a card fell out of some books. As he looked up smiling, handing the card to me, I almost cried. It was an old Christmas card from Grandpa Bill.

We had no idea how or why the card might have ended up behind some books in our bedroom, but I looked up to the sky and said, "Thank you, Grandpa, for the Christmas card."

I called my mom right away to tell her, and we agreed that Grandpa couldn't use the normal post office anymore, so he had sent a card to me this way. We hung it proudly with all the other cards we received that year.

In that holiday Season of light, I was so grateful looking back, thinking of how in my darkest hours it wasn't just one person or place helping me, but a colorful patchwork quilt of many different aspects; God, angels, life experiences, friends, family, spirit guides, animals, nature, the places I have lived and visited, religious teachings, and love. As colorful and varied as a giant quilt, these influences comforted, protected and delivered me across the void to a newer and better life. Maybe one day, I will make a physical representation of this quilt, so when I am old and weak and preparing to leave this Earth, the blanket can warm and comfort me in my final hours; so I remember.

And why, you may ask, did my angels not stop the terrible injury from happening to my neck? Maybe it was because they knew if it didn't happen I wouldn't have found this new life that unfolded in front of me or marry a new wonderful husband. Maybe they knew I would have missed out on all the great people and adventures of a beautiful life in Montana, while becoming closer to many of my family members. I just have to trust that perhaps my fate would have been far worse if I had stayed in California near my threatening ex-husband. It seems angels and spirits that help and guide our lives have a more far-reaching view than us humans, who can only see a little sliver of the world and universe at any one time. I have to thank them for all they did for me even while living with a chronic spinal issue. I had no idea then, but by not saving me from a traumatic event, they showed overflowing grace and love for my future.

EVEN WITH ALL MY new lessons learned, a humble heart, and ethereal philosophies, I sometimes still feel as out of place in my new home as a mermaid in the mountains. Then, I am reminded, as I throw a winter hat on my shell-entwined mermaid hair and mittens on my iridescent hands, how I found myself in the least likely of places, and realize it's *exactly* where I belong.

And when the many feet of snow blow down from the crystal-laden, shivering mountains, and cover our home, I grab a hiking pole, tuck my mermaid fins into snow boots, and happily open the frigid, ice-encrusted, front door. Out we walk, down our slick cement steps, along the path recently cleared of snow by John. Sunny dog happily follows behind in his snazzy coat and boots, as we step into the windy, winter, Montana day, in this strange place, where once I thought I was so cold and in pain that I could not survive, and now I *thrive*, happy and alive.

Mahalo ke ala ke kua

C.M. Arvish

C.M. Arvish is the author of ***Mermaid In The Mountains.*** She grew up in the tropics and later migrated to a little island in the Northwest. She is the daughter of a bar owning, world traveling dad; a rebellious, nature-loving mom, and the great-granddaughter of a powerful hands-on healer. She is an author, muralist, and artist. She now lives in the mountains, with her loved ones, and two fuzzy babies.

Like us at Facebook.com/mermaid in the mountains_book.

Follow us @Mermaid In The Mountains_book on Twitter.

ACKNOWLEDGMENTS

My warmest Alohas and sincere mahalo to the Earth Mother and Father God, nature spirits, angels, and otherworldly beings, for protecting and guiding me along a crazy and sometimes harrowing journey. Much admiration, praise, and thanks to my wonderful editors Jorie Tash and K.W. Many thanks to my publishers, The Colorful Quill, in association with Amazon and Kindle.

I offer gratitude to my friends and family, and much love to my husband John for your unwavering support. You are one of the greatest gifts in my life. I give my heartfelt thanks to Kelsey, the best friend anyone could have, who knows everything about me and still loves me. I can never thank Sunny dog enough, for his sweet angelic spirit, empathetic heart, and joyous smiles, which warmed me through the darkest nights. Mahalo, for all the encouraging, funny, and nourishing comments throughout this process.

My love for the Islands that I grew up on is strong and enduring, but I am thankful for finding peace and love in the wild mountains.

I sincerely appreciate and acknowledge some of my teachers such as my English teacher David Guterson, (author of *Snow Falling on Cedars)*, for your tutelage and inspiration. To my exuberant creative writing teacher, Mr. McAlister, (RIP), I thank you for all of your encouragement and energy.

A big mahalo to my parents; who always gave me the freedom to express my creativity and the independent spirit to pursue my goals. A huge thanks goes out to my adventure dad who pushed me through some hair-raising events even when I was a chicken. Thanks to Carla A. for your child-like enthusiasm and for being a constant cheerleader. I can't forget Jimmers P. and Jenny F. for all your praise, joy, and encouragement.

And, last but not least, Thank you, Elise, for your kind and inspirational ways.

Aloha Nui Loa

Remember, you are so much more than
they think you are, so keep shining!

Mahalo for the line in this song that goes something like this, "Although I am broken, my heart is still untamed."

Story of My Life by One Direction—Midnight Memories (Deluxe Edition)

Music and books referenced in

MERMAID IN THE MOUNTAINS

MUSIC

"Father Figure" by George Michael

"First Gymnopedie" by Erik Satie

"Let it Fade" by Jeremy Camp

"Story of My Life" by One Direction —Midnight Memories (Deluxe Edition)

"Tupelo Honey" by Cassandra Wilson and Van Morrison

"True Companions" by Marc Cohn

BOOKS

The Woman with the Alabaster Jar, Margaret Starbird.

The Mystical Life of Jesus: An Uncommon Perspective on the Life of Christ, Sylvia Browne.

The Great Goddess: Reverence of the Divine Feminine from the Paleolithic to the Present, Jean Markale.

I Ching, unknown author.

Amulets of the Goddess: Oracle of Ancient Wisdom, Nancy Blair.

If you would like to try "The Best Cheesecake in the World," in my humble opinion, the recipe is available in the following pages.

My maiden name, as it relates to the story and Rhode Island is Budlong.

"THE BEST CHEESECAKE IN THE WORLD"
Like Grandma Used To Make
(Adapted from family and friend's recipes)

First things first
A homemade, with love, graham cracker pie crust.

ingredients
1 ½ cups finely ground graham cracker crumbs.
Add coconut, or a splash of cinnamon, for a little extra spark.
(1 ¼ cup graham cracker crumbs to ¼ cup coconut works
great)
1/3 cup white sugar
7-8 tablespoons butter, melted

Directions
1. Mix graham cracker crumbs, sugar,
   melted butter and (cinnamon/coconut if added)

until well blended.
2. Press mixture into a 9-inch springform pan, pushing it all the way up the side rim. The filling will puff up.
3. Bake at 375 degrees Fahrenheit for 7 minutes. Cool.

All done! Now time to add the amazing, delicious, creamy innards.

Filling ingredients

2 (8 ounce) packages of cream cheese, softened.
Add some more love, sewing projects, garden flowers to the dining room table, and sandy saltwater sandals to the deck. *Next!*
1 cup of sugar
2-3 tablespoons lemon juice
1 teaspoon vanilla
A dash of salt
4 eggs (from the wacky neighbor down the lane with chickens, whenever possible)

Directions

1. Preheat oven to 325 degrees Fahrenheit.
2. In a bowl, combine the cream cheese, sugar, lemon juice, vanilla & salt.
3. Mix on low with a blender until smooth and well blended. (Add the eggs after this step to avoid lumps)
4. Add eggs, one at a time, mixing well after each addition.
5. Place your already made graham crust on a baking sheet; pour in filling.
6. Bake 60 minutes or until knife inserted comes out clean. (It should be puffed up, not sinking in the middle).
7. Take pleasure in taunting those around you with the amazing cooking smells coming from the kitchen.

The All Important Topping!

1 ½ cups sour cream (full fat, don't skimp on this one)
3 tablespoons sugar
1 teaspoon vanilla
Have some of Grandma's homemade canned jams available,
but if not, make the most delicious fruit compote you can.
Warm it up, to make it extra special.

Directions

1. Combine sour cream, 2 tablespoons sugar and
   ¼ teaspoon vanilla in a bowl. Blend on low.
2. Carefully spread over pie innards after the 60 minutes of
   baking is up.
3. Continue baking 10 more minutes. Cool.

Cool

Chill long enough to go for a rowboat ride and look down at
goofy eyed flounder, walk along the shore beachcombing, ride
a bike, sing to yourself while kayaking to the rhythm of the
paddle strokes, or whatever strikes your fancy.

Display

Set atop a pie platform made of crystal with flowers on the
side.

Serve

Place on pretty plates with dainty designs, or on eclectic mix-
matched patterns. Who's kidding! I would eat it out of an old
clamshell if given the chance.

But most of all enjoy!!!

Thank you to the singers and songwriters, for giving a voice to God's unconditional love. And Mahalo to the radio stations in Helena, and Missoula, Montana, for broadcasting these inspirational songs and turning my sticker-covered, hippie-mobile, into a rolling worship center.

I listed many of my favorite songs, but there are many, many more unlisted, but still very much appreciated.

"Babe In the Straw" by Caedmon's Call

"Better For It" by Riley Clemmons

"Born Again" by Austin French

"Brand New" by Ben Rector

"Broken Things" by Matthew West

"Bulletproof" Citizen Way

"Chain Reaction" by River Valley Worship

"Changed" by Jordan Feliz

"Counting Every Blessing" by Rend Collective

"Cover the Earth" (Live) by Kari Jobe & Cody Carnes

"Even Then" by Micah Tyler

"Everything" by Lincoln Brewster

"Details" by Sarah Reeves

"Faithfulness" by Matt Maher

"Fierce" Jesus Culture

"Finally Free" by Rend Collective

"Freedom" Jesus Culture

"Freedom Hymn" by Austin French

"Ghost" by Ella Henderson

"God of Wonders" by Mac Powell, Cliff Young & Danielle
Young

"God Only Knows" by for KING & COUNTRY

"Gold" by Apollo LTD

"Good Hands" by Finding Faith

"Gospel Medley" by Lizz Wright

"Grace Got You" by MercyMe

"Great Are You Lord" by one sonic society

"Hallelujah" by Heather Williams

"Heaven on Earth" by Stars Go Dim

"Here With Us" by Joy Williams

"How Many Kings" by Downhere

"I just need U" by TobyMac

"Impossible" by Sidewalk Prophets

"I NeedYou God" by Consumed by Fire

"Inside Out" by Bonray

"In the Water" by GAWVI

"Isaac" by Hollyn

"joy" by for KING & COUNTRY

"Known" by Tauren Wells

"Let Them See You" by JJ Weeks Band

"Light of the World" by Lauren Daigle

"Messengers" by Lecrae

"Multiplied" by NEEDTOBREATHE

"My Story" by Big Daddy Weave

"Not Today" by Hillsong UNITED

"Oh Fear" by Moriah Peters

"One Step Away" by Casting Crowns

"Open Up the Heavens" by Meredith Andrews

"Overwhelmed" by Big Daddy Weave

"Radiate" by Hannah Kerr

"Reckless love" by Cory Asbury

"Right on Time" by Aaron Cole

"Rise" by Danny Gokey

"Rise Up" by Andra Day

"So Will I" by Hillsong UNITED

"So Will I" by Hillsong Worship

"Story Teller" by Morgan Harper Nichols

"TellYour Heart To Beat Again" by Danny Gokey

"The Greatest" by Sia

"The Prayer" by Danny Gokey & Natalie Grant

"There is Power" by Lincoln Brewster

"The River" by Jordan Feliz

"Throne Room" by Kim Walker-Smith

"Touch The Sky" by Hillsong UNITED

"Tremble" by Mosaic MSC

"Walk on Waves" by Austin & Lindsey Adamec

"What a Beautiful Name" by Hillsong Worship

"When We Pray" by Tauren Wells

"Who You Say I Am (Live) by Hillsong Worship

"Wings" by Live, —Songs From Black Mountain

Discussion questions and topics

1. In *Mermaid In The Mountains,* otherworldly communications, guidance, and protection from angels and spirit guides play an important role. Has anyone here ever had an angel, ghost, or spirit encounter? If so, what was it and how did it impact your life?

2. C.M. Arvish had to face a death threat and make an emergency escape plan. Has anyone here ever had to take steps to escape or make an emergency exit route from something or someone?

3. Adventures abound in many foreign counties—some comical, gross, and poignant—while C.M. Arvish and several colorful characters relay their experiences abroad. Please share any adventures close to home, or in other countries. Did these experiences influence your way of thinking about different cultures and people?

4. Some very special and heartfelt relationships with animals are revealed in *Mermaid In The Mountains.* Has anyone here had a significant relationship or bond with an animal? How has this positively affected your life?

5. Every group of family or friends has that one (or more) people in their lives that challenge, entertain, or baffle them. Do you have any strange, fantastic, or eclectic friends or family members?

6. C.M. Arvish's life is transformed dramatically in *Mermaid In The Mountains.* Has anyone here had a dramatic shift or surprise occurrence that altered their reality, or life as they know it?

Made in the USA
Columbia, SC
20 February 2020